# Low Cost High Life

## Live an affordable life of Luxury

**By Mark Homer**
The Contrarian Capitalist

"The (life) story of real wealth creation through a tight fisted approach to investing from a tight fisted investor. Someone who gets the highest pleasure out of the lowest cost, high life" – Rob Moore

# www.progressiveproperty.co.uk

Order this book online at www.progressiveproperty.co.uk
or on Amazon and in Waterstones or email mark.homer@progressiveproperty.co.uk

Other books by Rob Moore and Mark Homer can be ordered at
www.progressiveproperty.co.uk

Note for Librarians: A cataloguing record for this book is available from Library and Archives Canada at www.collections Canada.ca/amicus/index-e.html

A catalogue record for this book is available from the British Library: ISBN: 978-1-909846-70-8

Printed in Peterborough, Cambridgeshire, UK

ISBN: 978-1-909846-70-8
www.progressiveproperty.co.uk
Progressive House
Unit 9 Forder Way
Cygnet Park
Peterborough
PE7 8GX
01733 898550
ask@progressiveproperty.co.uk
Skype: mark.progressive

# Foreword

In business and property, have your dream or your end result and then see another dream in the distance; focus day by day and eventually you will get to that dream. Mark is proof of that. In business one of the most important factors is to focus and you will soon be surprised that the more you focus the more answers you can come up with.

There are two types of people in this world; one that has their dreams while they're asleep and the other who realises their dreams while they're awake. Finally, working should be a pleasure not a chore. Every problem you face in business should not be looked upon as a problem but a situation and every situation should be looked upon as an opportunity. Mark is one of the few who has gone out there and done it and this book will show you a realistic way that you can be successful too.

**Andreas Panayiotou**

(Owned 8,000+ residential properties before selling at the top of the market in 2006)

# About Mark Homer

Mark Homer became a financially free businessman investor by the time he was in his early 30's. He has built a portfolio of companies and almost 300 properties in his extended partner property portfolio. In this unique book he shows you in his renowned analytical, detailed and controversially skeptical nature how you can realistically achieve the low cost high life for the long term, in the shortest possible timeframe. Mark will show you in a direct, disdainfully dismissive of scams and schemes manner how to live an affordable life of luxury which is sustainable for the long term and not just riding the crest of a property boom. This book presents in relentless detail:

- How to use 'silent compounding,' to turn small daily savings anyone can make, into large chunks of lifetime cash

- How to keep exactly the same lifestyle you have now and 'spend invest,' your way to a minimum of £1,791,735 in 20 years or less, proven and detailed in this book

- The 'Giant leap' wealth attraction strategy using everyday 'household,' items and hidden daily opportunities to make long term cash and passive recurring income

- The 'Wealth mirage' technique to create and live a high opulent lifestyle on minimum daily costs and savings

- How to use low/no cost fast-start tactics such as 'Gratitude Leverage,' and 'Cheek creativity,' to get others to do what you want, when you want, for the low cost high life

- 'Irregular shock protection,' 'Liquid cash pile power,' and 'Random cash windfalls,' for the easy way to the low cost, high life affordable life of luxury

So let's get started…

# Contents

# 1. Introduction

Life is getting more and more expensive. Cost of living keeps going up at a higher rate then the inflation figures suggest, pensions have dwindled and are taking longer and longer to pay out, and people are having to work more and longer for the same (or lower) quality of life. People are having more children than ever, divorce statistics are alarmingly high, and post apocalyptic recession has left many businesses having to start again. Technology is moving at a faster and faster rate, and people at the lower level, operational employment level are being replaced by computers, drones and robotics. The gap between the rich and poor is compounding more than ever and while Roman Abramovich is commissioning the biggest non commercial Yacht/mini Ferry, unemployment is only just starting to stabilize.

These Darwinian financial times are a real danger to those who are uneducated about wealth management and money. But they are a huge opportunity for well educated, innovative and disruptive Entrepreneurs like you and I. This book is my 25 year voyeuristic journey on how I view the pursuit of business, property and wealth in these most unique times. Apparently I have quite an eccentric (but proven to work) view of creating wealth; through a low cost base and having a 'tight-fisted,' (coined by others, especially my partner Gemma) approach to most investments and purchases. Though of course this is normal to me. I've lived a colourful life, especially in my early days where I got experiences in different countries around the world which shaped my investing and business outlook. Many have said I have a non standard, contrarian view to investment which has come about from my earliest mentor, my father, who was tighter than a Duck's arse, and, as they say, that's waterproof.

There's also been a lot of trial and error and other mentors along the way who've guided me to live a low cost, high life, and afford a life of (apparently) luxury on an eye watering-ly tight budget. From a standing start I have, before 30 years old and with the help of my business partner Rob, built multiple companies, intentionally from scratch, that now employ upwards of 40 people. We have an interest in or directly own around 300 properties with a gross value of £25M+ and have trained tens of thousands of people through our property investment training company. Our combined group turnover is in the multiple millions (excluding property rental income).

This is the story of the path that led me here and my hope is that as well as finding it interesting you will get some ready to use pointers on how to grow your empire at extremely low cost. I despise wasting money. In fact I despise spending money, and this addiction-disease I intend to pass onto you so you can build your 'low cost, high life' on a miserly budget, living the most luxurious life that people will scratch their heads in confusion at. Nothing will feel better than to know that 'every pound was your prisoner,' and that you wasted not a single penny in your attainment of your 'affordable life of luxury.' Oh yes. Or Ohhhhh YES! (you will find out the weird meaning of this later in the book).

I've always been interested, fascinated and addicted to the no Bullshit reality of business and money, and have incessantly looked to cut through all the noise, fluff, distraction, get rich quick, scams and schemes in order to discover the real, proven and sustainable systems and super long term strategies to real wealth and business success. Anything else is simply a distraction or longer path to your dream.

I hope to be able to check in with you in some years to come with your low cost, compounded success and some big numbers. My life is still a work in progress as I only started properly in business in my early teens, and I have another 50 to 70 years of compounding to benefit from.

# 2. Early memories and 'being drilled' the fundamentals

Living in the Far East with Dad [Stuart] in Indonesia gave me some of my earliest memories of learning to invest. Dad was a consultant and was always employed or self employed. Born in WW2 time, things were not plentiful, living under strict rationing. These conditions shaped him into having VERY extreme cost cutting and saving mentality, and as you will discover, much of that rubbed off on me.

When he was 30 he got his first overseas posting in Iran. Working for the Overseas Development Aid arm for the British Government, he realised he could live out there and earn multiples of what he could at home, not pay a lot of tax, and save 80% of his salary. People wouldn't look at him as though he was strange because with a white face in a completely different culture he didn't fit in anyway, it suited Dad just fine not to fit in. Frequently telling me to 'be different,' he shunned many things 'imposed on him' by others. He was very much anti-establishment, and gained real pleasure from it. He could live like a King in countries like Iran, with servants, and have a great social life, on a much lower cost base than the UK. (He loved it, was an oddball and never fitted into English society anyway). His position and standing was elevated at a fraction of the cost or earnings required.

After being born in Singapore whilst living in Surabaya, Indonesia's second city, my earliest memories of living abroad came later.

My Dad had formed an extreme ex-pat persona and it became so ingrained that he couldn't live in the UK anymore, He wore flip-flops everywhere, distastefully loose shorts on with no underpants (ever) and a proud member of a running club called "Hash-house Harriers;" 'runners' in the loose sense: more about drinking, rebellion against the conventional and general quirky or bad behaviour. He'd wear his Hash

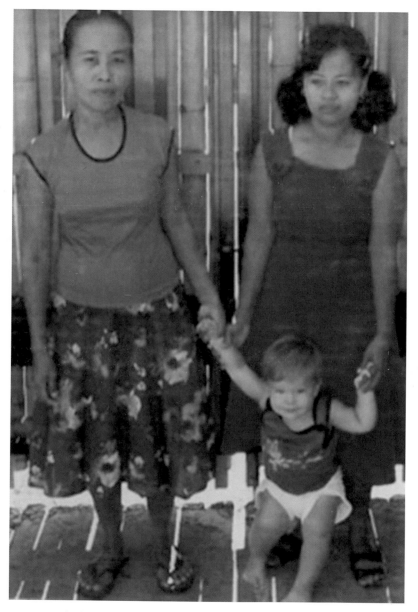

A picture of me with our 2 local pembantu (Maids) in earlier years.

A picture of mum and Dad on a Hash run in his signature kit!

T-shirts frequently like a form of medal.

By the time I was 8 years old he'd lived in 15 countries, dragging my Mum around like a battered piece of luggage – all through Africa and the Middle East. He got very used to the extremely low cost of living – sometimes $1/10^{th}$ of the cost of the UK. Getting used to paying 10p for a Coffee or £3 for dinner has an effect on your appreciation of what 'value for money' is. I didn't appreciate for many years how this was forming my gaggin-reflex to spending money.

He became a very good entertainer with all his stories of life overseas, and because he was such an oddball people would want to hang their marshmallows over the fire and listen to the fables. But it was very embarrassing to me.

After having moved back to the UK from Surabaya, I went to a local primary school just outside Birmingham in Halesowen. Dad owned a new-ish house that he'd bought some years before, and even 5 years after buying it there was still no carpet down and we'd walk around on untreated floorboards with splinters everywhere. Dad thought carpets were an 'unnecessary expense' and cost 'silly money.' We were going to be moving anyway, so it would be an extravagant expense (we'd been there 5 years!).

We had entirely $2^{nd}$ hand furniture, including mattresses, and a Mini which Dad kept pristine in the Garage. Mum had to get on her cycle or catch the Bus to work because Dad didn't want any miles or dirt on the Mini. That car received more love than my Mum and was more of a museum relic than a practical vehicle.

During this part of my life Dad was living in Sierra Leone and Tanzania, whist Mum and I stayed in the UK. Once he brought back some precious stones for Mum and he'd hidden them in some Loudspeakers he was bringing in so he didn't have to pay out 'silly money' in duty to get them back into the UK.

I attended the local state primary school at 6, perhaps not the place that I got most out of in terms of developing my outlook. As characterised by many of my school years, I got myself into plenty of trouble, frequently waiting outside the headmasters office. My Dad's family lived close by and I think my cousins were equally troublesome so I didn't look as abnormal. My Nan worked as a teacher and Granddad ran the sawmill at Longbridge, the Austin factory.

Thinking back my Dad turned into a bit of both of these two careers of a teacher and an automotive engineer that his parents had as he ended up running training facilities for multinational companies often based around mechanical items such as Cars.

Life was pretty basic and stripped back growing up, and virtually everything had to be done on an OCD tight-fisted budget. Mum tried hard to save for luxuries for us that Dad thought were unnecessary and give me what she thought kids should get regardless of Dads ways. Dad believed that virtually everything should be bought on a 'deal.' Or 'below market value,' as we say in the property world. He bought a large supply of Chocolate from a chap on the market which was way past its best before date, 'still tastes fine to me,' Dad said. Toothpaste must be rolled tightly from the end, squeezing every last drop out. Any tubes thrown away which were not completely crushed would result in a reprimand. Dad thought that bottled water was one of the biggest cons in the world today and laughed at the people who bought it; 'whats wrong with council water from the tap!?' Starbucks was another source of amusement, £3 for a Coffee!? CRAZY people; 'what's wrong with 50p from the Danish Invader?' (a rough local pub).

Life was, however, punctuated by periods of excitement when Dad would act in an outlandish fashion, often when he would return from one of his stints in Africa. We would go out to visit, like one of the trips to Dar es Salaam in Tanzania when Dad took me out in a Leyland fire truck which he had just bought a fleet of for the Tanzanian government. We rode round town with the blue lights flashing and siren/air horn going ensuring fast passage through town. Such was life out there at this time that this was considered normal behaviour by my Dad's mates in the local police force. It was audacious and rebellious and Dad loved it; and I think perhaps some of this rubbed out on me later as I found it harder and harder to accept authority and saw benefit in Contrarianism.

When back in the UK, Dad would take me up to the Rugby club in the Mini where they had a big open car park. He would teach me to drive, and being at 8 years old, I totally loved it. Of course he'd be really fussy about what I touched and where we drove so as to keep the Mini pristine, but I loved the opportunity to do something different that other people my age couldn't do.

Being an automotive engineer and employed in the Car industry before I was born, Dad knew everything about cars and planes. He would frequently teach me how car mechanicals worked, how to change oil, tyres and he loved trying new equipment out. He taught me upon buying my first car, a brown Vauxhall Nova for £37 plus auction fee that I did 65,000 miles in, how to change the oil and manually do the service and it would cost less than £7.

Dad's time with me would often be us in bed under the covers as he would run through the Concorde take off checklist – 'taxiing out onto the runway, full power, V1, rotate making all of the noises;' we used to have some great times getting all technical and detailed. I didn't realise that 'normal' kids played sport and stuff.

In 1987 Dad got a new contract working for Hoff and Overgaard, a Danish consulting company in Indonesia. He managed to sell the house (with no carpet) only a few months before the market plummeted, right at the top (he maintained this was the only time he had ever managed this with any asset and it was very much luck rather than judgment). The job was for 2-3 years and with a lot of excitement we left for Jakarta so that he could start his new job.

## Obsessive compulsive & tight-fisted

When we arrived in Jakarta, Indonesia we got a house that was half as good as everyone else's on Dad's salary level in the company. He was paying around US$800 per month for our house, where most of the other families were paying US$2,000 a month. I hated it because it was old, not refurbished for 30 years, horrible dark wood and stunk of Rentokil spray used to kill the cockroaches. It had no garden, was built on a postage stamp and had very loud "window" style air conditioning. Dad filled it (as empty a 'filling,' as you could get) with 30 year-old furniture. We had a 25 year old Toyota Corona, with a local driver. This sounds opulent, but instead of getting a trained driver with a license, which was standard for ex-pats, he'd pull someone out of a local poor village called a Kampung, teach them to drive himself, and then Mum would take it upon herself to buy the poor souls (we had a few leave!) some clothes and teach them general hygiene to avoid stinking the car out. He'd then pay them £7 a week which even for Indonesia in 1988 was really cheap!

Dad would make the driver keep a log of every kilometer he did in the Car. For every journey, the driver (on virtually no earnings) would have to write a start of journey mileage and then end of journey mileage (even just to the local shops), along with estimated fuel consumption. Fuel usage was then checked against the mileage log for fuel syphoning. Fuel was cheap in Indonesia in those days; £10 for a tank for a car like this, but Dad wanted to save every drop, and was certainly not going to have any of our drivers syphoning fuel at my Dad's expense.

Once, Dad worked out that the driver had been using the radio whilst on his own in the car and changing the frequency, which he disliked because he thought it messed the station presets and balance/tone of the speakers. He was very obsessive about anything he owned and thought that the driver didn't know how to use it (a cheap radio on a 25 year old car) properly. So one Saturday morning he took me down to 'block M,' the local electronics market, and bought a key switch, which we fitted behind the dashboard while I was made to watch and help pass the tools. Dad was very pleased with himself now, and any driver then needed a key to turn the radio on, which of course the driver didn't have, and they couldn't touch/damage his 25 year old radio or alter the tone or preset stations.

On occasions that Dad drove the Car, he'd be labouring the engine in 5th gear at 20 miles an hour to save fuel: 1st, 2nd then quickly up into 5th. He rarely went over 55 or 60mph. Bear in mind that he was earning around £40K per year, paying no tax, back in the late 80's; giving it around a £100K net equivalent today. He must have spent no more that £15K of that £100K, and he agonised over fuel that was very very cheap. Once a year or so he would open the taps and drive the car like he stole it when we were having fun or he had been annoyed by something. Then back to 60 tops for the other 364 days.

Later, when we came back to the UK in my early teenage years, Dad hired on a long term deal a Yugo Sana, a Yugoslavian Astra sized car built from a Russian parts bin. By this time I was attending Oakham school, a public school, and Dad was driving me to the school gates in this cold war relic. I will never forget when Alex assembled 5 other kids on the top floor, looking out the window as my Dad drove up Wharflands drive, pointing at my Dad and laughing. I had been completely ridiculed. I should have been used to this, but I hated it every time.

We were always travelling around, and if my Dad bought a suitcase he wanted 25 good solid years of well travelled use out of it! He had a local seamstress make covers for each of his cases, which created a huge rigmarole having to put them on and take them off each time you filled or emptied the cases, just so the 'bastard' baggage handlers wouldn't ruin his beloved cases. What was worse for me was how ridiculous they looked, made out of cheap canvas like you'd see shielding a really old couple on a beach in Cromer. We looked ridiculous yet my Dad seemed to get some warped pleasure in being different, even if different was ridicule.

This obsession my Dad had with value drove much of my early experiences and understanding of money, especially drilling down costs. Although I like to think I have directed his ideas towards business and investing in a more productive way, I owe much of my understanding of money, its value and how to get the most out of every penny to him, and his fastidious attention on value and lifetime value, which I will talk about later in more detail as an important investment concept.

Later I shall detail the difference between appreciating assets and depreciating liabilities, but for now the main concept is to get 'maximum lifetime value,' out of a product, service or investment. Short term opportunism might make a fast buck, but in the long term will probably be a relic of the past and end up either costing not making money, or the return will diminish instead of compound upwards. I look for stocks that will last my lifetime, I buy assets (especially property) that will exceed my lifetime, and if there is a necessity to buy depreciating assets, I want pre-depreciated, maximum lifetime value, to get the best return on capital employed, or to have spent/wasted the least amount of capital so I can re invest it in appreciating assets. A lifetime of appreciation or minimised depreciation compounds to significant wealth over time, and preserves cash; up there with oxygen and spreadsheets as my most favourite concept.

## Non conformism – it's them

Dads 'Hash,' shorts given to him as promotional items through his club or from companies looking to sponsor their products, for free of course, were worn to death. He'd never wear pants, and his testicles would frequently drop out the side of them, normally and frustratingly for me whilst having meetings or at social occasions and in my full view. People would often sit and stare in disbelief. My Mum would declare, 'Stuart, you're showing,' but I don't think he really cared. 'That's their problem,' he'd say, and nonchalantly place whichever testicle had freed itself back upwards, and carry on, business as usual. Dad always believed that the rest of the world was too conformist and that *they* were the ones with the funny ideas. At the time I was really embarrassed but I see the funny side now.

*(NOW) Although not at my father's level, non-conformism can often be profitable. Not necessarily a great strategy in your personal dress or intimate relationships, but doing the opposite of the masses,' will usually pay you better in the long term than herd-ism. If the world is buying a share it's probably not right or had its day, if you have 12 investors all swarming around a buy to let you'll get priced up or out, and if you implement 'investing,' strategies of the masses, you'll never generate serious, lasting wealth. I have learned from Dad that questioning the norm is a good thing, and having a contrarian, non-conformist investing mentality (and portfolio) will mostly yield well. Extreme non-conformism however is a risk, and I feel my Dad's extreme behaviours restricted him in many ways, especially in happiness and relationships.*

*Dad's eccentricities drilled into me that just because others were getting nice houses and spending what the company paid them on nice Cars and the like, didn't mean that it was the right thing to do. Delaying gratification meant that you have more cash saved and to invest with, to create a more sustainable, recession proof future.*

## Principles, habits & crusts

Even when Dad was creating a training centre to train 2,000 people for a new Poly-ethylene (plastic) factory for BP in Indonesia, near the top of his career in the early 90's, we'd still only ever be allowed to go to a Pizza Hut on a Saturday PM as a real treat. Dad would do his structural calculations on the salad bowls so he could pile the salad as high as possible to maximise cost-benefit, and strategically plan evasion so they couldn't charge him for a second visit [rough cost £1]. We were ONLY EVER allowed tap water, absolutely no fizzy drinks, and any over-ordering would result in chastisement. Anything left by Mum or myself would result in Dad eating it in front of us exclaiming with a mouth full of Pizza crust: 'You must never waste anything, ever.' Every now and again he'd get caught having a second trip to the salad bar which would result in him being quite happy to obstinately defend his position of only paying for one trip. Sometimes for ten minutes (that would seem like hours), insisting 'that rule only applied to overweight Chinese-Indonesian's who abuse the salad bar.' My Mum would try to walk away during these episodes, and I'd feel totally embarrassed, for me and for her; she hated it too. I couldn't understand why he would go through all of that to save what seemed like such a small amount. 'False economy' was certainly a theme that ran through my childhood. Dad would spend three hours to save £3, effectively valuing his time at zero. The reality was that he could have used this time way more productively to generate income rather than solely (and in such an extreme way) focusing on cost saving. I have had to wean myself off this habit and am much freer with small amounts of cash than I was and fiercely defensive of my time.

## Policing the Police

Once every few months one of the local traffic Police standing on their vantage point would spot my Dad pulling a minor infringement, such as not indicating, and would pull him over. They often did this to foreigners, and a 'small donation,' of around £3, which was seen as standard procedure, was 'expected,' and the infringement would be overlooked. This would be nothing to us, but half a week's wages to them.

My Dad would not have this. He would stand firm and relentless argue his corner, even knowing he was in the wrong, often for more than half an hour a time, until they broke and backed down. One specific occasion he came up against a particularly steadfast officer who wanted his 10,000 Rupiah, and Dad sat there arguing with him for over an hour, until even this officer gave in and let him on his way without payment. Neither Mum nor I could understand why he would kick up such a stink. Even worse was the stench and silence for a good long while afterwards in the car, between us and Dad, because we would have to cancel what we were going to do that day because of all the wasted time, and Dad would be angry for the rest of the day. This frequently seemed to happen when we were supposed to be going out as a family.

Dad deviously managed to find a way around these annoyances by cozying up to the head of the Jakarta traffic police; Tommy Sobango, who Dad met once a week at his Hash running club. As soon as he had the chance to meet him, Dad was all over it, and him, even ensuring his testicles stayed in his shorts. I remember him coming home saying 'everything is now sorted son. We can now get across town quickly and no more traffic fines will come our way.' He was particularly smug and excited about this result, and the defiance and victory.

From that point on, as soon as we'd get pulled over, my Dad would come out with his standard line, in Indonesian: 'Every Monday evening I have a meeting with my pal Tommy, you know Tommy…' and at this point the Policemen's faces would always drop, 'and you can telephone him for confirmation.' Needless to say none of them did, they would tip their cap and wave him on.

On special occasions should the need arise to get through the horrendous Jakarta traffic, Dad would take great pleasure in telling his mates how Tommy would dispatch an outrider with a blue light to clear the traffic.

*(NOW) Although Dad's reasons were typically eccentric, Dad's desire to get on side with Tommy taught me the importance of building a great network. I didn't really understand why he went to such great lengths to schmooze Tommy, but later realised that Tommy opened doors for Dad and gave him an easier route to status and results, in reality and by association. From an early age I learned the importance of building a network of powerful, knowledgeable and well-connected people, not to get waved through rush hour, but to help build your business and investments faster and learn strategies and tactics 'lesser mortals,' never understood. My Dad really believed this, and despite his skinflint tendencies, put me through private school in some part for this reason I think.*

## Trafficking

I remember a trip to Australia from Indonesia, and Dad got stopped at the airport for having an Apple in his bag; not allowed in Australia. The customs officer wanted to throw it away, and Dad, being typically 'Stuart,' as my Mum would say, grabbed the Apple off him and ate it in front of him so he couldn't have it. Mum said she wanted to curl up at the time. 'Totally ridiculous wasting good food like that,' Dad said.

Mum used to find Dad excessive and knew that his tendencies needed tempering. I think she appreciated his brilliance with people, he could entertain people very effectively in a social setting and for passing on some great qualities to me, but she tried to show me that Dad's bad side didn't need to be replicated. When he was engaging in one of his little moments she would often pull me aside to stop it rubbing off. Your judgment or time will tell if she achieved this.

## Tax avoidance (literally)

And then there was my Dad's tax affairs. Dad believed that living in England needed to be avoided for a number of reasons such has the weather, lack of opportunity, backward opinions and tax.

For thirty years he managed to stay out of the country for the required period every year, allowing him to completely disengage in paying any UK tax, which he was very proud of. The reality was that he hadn't used any of the services, NHS or the like for decades, so as well as being legally OK it would have been OK by most people's moral compass anyway.

This didn't stop him from being totally neurotic about the mere mention of the Inland Revenue, who he thought had horns and the sole intention of destroying his hard work overseas. Dad believed that wealth creation was an essential endeavour, and needed to become integral to who I grew up to be. He certainly believed however that this should be done in a quiet way, and that no one should be able to get a clear handle on how much you make or have made. Dad thought that the more people knew, the more power they could wield over you and try to take your wealth from you. He was a believer in turning up and looking like he was the poorest man in the room, knowing inside that he was probably the richest. He loved this concept.

*(NOW) This certainly rubbed off on me, and gratuitous opulence flaunted all over the place is something not instilled in me, and not in keeping with the low cost high life values. Rob, my business partner, enjoys sales and*

*marketing and training, but as I write this I have even surprised myself that I am revealing my wealth creation strategies in a book. I have been a private person when it comes to the revealing of wealth, and I think this is the right thing to do. You never know who's watching, and some people may envy you or feel threatened if you flaunt your wealth.*

*This aside, as my years in business have progressed, I've learned that you should not worry about being judged, and do what you want to do. I had almost a dozen investment properties and still lived at home with Mum & William to keep costs down, and Rob still teases me about this to this day. I probably have taken this a little far at times, so strike the right balance between doing what you want to do without fear of being judged, but understand if you flaunt it then you risk that others will come digging.*

## Summary

The road to riches was instilled in my early life. The foundation of value, never paying full price (discount to value) was a concept I learned from Dad and took it a step further during my later years of property investing. Investing was something I wanted to do even before I knew anything about 'value' investing. And it was never something I had to "learn" but grew up with. The importance of saving money at an early age and knowing the concept of receiving more value than the price paid was one of the most profound and important concepts I ever received. If you pay too much you get very little value, but if you pay too little then the value you receive is greatly increased. Knowing this difference will materially impact not only the rate of return the investor receives, but perhaps more importantly, the risk they take to get it.

## 3. Shoestring education

One thing my Dad did believe in was education. He believed that a good education was very important, and this was one of the *very* few things he didn't mind spending money on. His extreme behaviours meant that he had enough money in one savings account to pay my £12k PA school fees just from the highest interest rates of the mid 90s. Impressive from someone who worked as a consultant and never earned much more than £100,000 (or today's inflation adjusted equivalent) in any one year.

*(NOW) This shows the power in the discipline to save with a long term view, and the power of 'silent compounding.'* We'll detail this later.

But he didn't like the costs that came with it. I'd turn up to school in jackets, trousers and sports kit a full 3 sizes too big 'good enough to last for the next 4 years.' You see my Dad's theory was that I needed '2 years to grow into them, one year at the right size and one year a bit tight.' The other kids really gave it to me about this, especially in the 1st and 4th year of the uniform life cycle. Most of the other kids at boarding school were from really wealthy families. Most of the bigger hitters had significant businesses and were rolling in it by my estimation. I developed a burning desire to live this life and watched through my teens how this could be achieved by following the example of many of my friend's Dad's. In many ways this desire grew from a feeling of embarrassment in that I didn't have what other kids did or the background that they had.

All of Dads embarrassing traits had lead me to keep him away from my school friends, especially in the bangers he used to drive. My friends didn't know him until much later, but the reality was that they found him pretty cool, so perhaps this was a mistake.

# Delaying gratification

Dad was *all* about delaying gratification. I think it was to do with his obsessive and controlling behaviour. I was surrounded in this environment and indoctrinated by it into a forced 'saving culture'. It meant I always had less to spend, but a warm feeling that my Piggy Bank had more in it than all the other kids. Nike Air Jordan's, Reebok Pumps, LA Gear's and shell suits were for the other kids. I guess I'm glad that the shell suits were for the other kids now :-) I had to make do with a pair of flip-flops and a good quality German satchel, because my Dad knew that German products were built to last.

My Dad believed that anything German was God-like. As an engineer he believed they were the greatest nation on earth. Many of his best friends were Germans, and he adopted many of their national stereotypes. He believed that if the world was run more like Germany, the world would be in a better place. I shall leave this point here, though.

I was bothered when young about not having what the other kids had, but I figured that I could work towards getting them. My Dad would set a specific savings goal towards the attainment of an item, but any misuse or loss of my existing possessions would put plans in complete jeopardy, so I had to be disciplined.

Frequently, after a long period of saving, I would end up getting the item I wanted, only to find that the reality didn't match the dream. I'd then, through choice, take the item back to obtain a refund. This made me more interested in the process of saving and acquiring wealth, rather than the spending of it; the dream was always better than the reality, but dreaming alone without actually having the wealth was fraudulent in Dads world so you had to make it first!

*(NOW) With hindsight, this was a very valuable lesson from my Dad. I doubt he was teaching me about gratitude, but it certainly built-in a sense of enjoyment in working towards a goal to attain or achieve something (especially financial). Enjoying the process of the investment goal, dividend or acquisition is what kept my life long, fire-burning excitement in business and investing. Even when I can easily afford the asset or depreciating liability, I like to invest in another asset to pay for it, to enjoy the sport and the process, preserve the vitally important capital, and maintain a grounded sense of pure enjoyment. I do not enjoy the sinking feeling where the attainment of the goal was too easy and therefore of little value, or not what I had pedestal- ised it as. A high life at minimum cost gives the great cost/benefit ratio.*

*I constantly see people buy what they don't need and then never use it. People buy clothes that hang in the wardrobe with the tags still on, buy things not fit for purpose because they didn't research properly, or buy new things that are shiny only to give them away, or for them not to last. If only they used my 'parallel universe thinking' technique and could see like a heads up display, all the wasted capital depreciating versus the compounded cash growing. Don't worry; we will be covering this technique at length later.*

## Maximum value

My upbringing had been reasonably hard with resources very controlled until I was 10, and it started to change when my Dad got a job with BP. Being an oil company, they were probably the most profitable and biggest spending organisation an ex-pat could work for at that time. They treated their employees like royalty, and when we moved back to Indonesia for this job, we were put up in a suite at the Borobudur Inter Continental Hotel for three months with all food, drink and bills fully paid for. This was to be fully leveraged by my Dad!

Every breakfast, lunch and dinner, I could have whatever I wanted. I could even take ad hoc visits to the Delicatessen in this sprawling 5 star hotel to consume whatever confectionary I desired at BP's expense. In typical Dad-like fashion, he managed to turn three months into more than six months, stretching the patience of the HR department, whilst he found the 'perfect,' house built to his ridiculous specifications.

We had a 2-bed apartment-suite with Kitchen, six telephones (even in the Bathrooms), four TV's with American channels, unlimited dry cleaning and unlimited use of the 8 restaurants in the hotel. Dad practically welded the cooker doors shut, and banned Mum from having anything in the fridge, so that he could reduce the housekeeping spend by using the hotels facilities, which were all free to us.

Other longer standing BP employees also lived in the Hotel and cottoned on to Dad's techniques and this gave Dad a bad reputation as a scrounger.

*[NOW] I now get a terrible feeling in my stomach if I feel that I am being seen as a scrounge, being unfair in a deal, or not paying my way. This is partly due to the embarrassment Dad created in those days, but also because of my Mum's beliefs around right and wrong. She believed that the way my Dad took advantage of people was wrong. This caused a lot of conflict between them. I'm not recommending some of my Dad's extreme behaviour, but can't deny I enjoyed BP's and Dad's joint venture in generosity.*

*Cost saving is advantageous when buying investments or, for example, doing refurbishments (refurbs), but detrimental in social and networking relationships. My Dad couldn't see the difference, but if you are a spendthrift around a potential higher network or in friendship circles, it can really hurt you. I really believe in giving generously to your friends and social circle, paying for dinners and excursions that add value to your relationships and being seen as one who is giving. I can see the difference between this and getting cheap flights or printers, and see network and social spending more as an investment that will yield a long term return, whereas Dad would have seen it as a cost.*

Dad virtually oversaw the build of our new house, had all the furniture built and employed 5 servants which BP paid for. Dad managed to wangle a newer Toyota Cressida that his grade didn't allow, through the back door, until the local Indonesian HR manager Irmwanto worked it out. Dad renamed him "Irmwanko."

*[NOW] Watching my Dad abuse spending when it wasn't his money, and spendthrifting to an anal-degree when it was his money, taught me how to assess spend/value ratio. When it isn't necessary to spend, where there will no be relative uplift in value or depreciation, it is really important to keep costs screwed right down Stuart Hash-pants style. 'Every pound is a prisoner,' and you want it staying in the bank or investment making money for you for LIFE. ONLY when you can guarantee uplift should you increase costs.*

## Summary

"The royal road to riches" where you get interest on interest from allowing returns to compound was a concept I learnt very early in life, which I adopted and didn't require vigilance, activity, or effort to make it work. Indeed, Einstein called compound interest the eighth wonder of the world. The correlation between the investor's ability to delay gratification—forgoing a smaller reward now for a larger reward in the future meant the better off they would be the earlier they learned this skill. These principles served me very well in property and other investment vehicles later on in life. Success leaves clues and investors should never be afraid to ask other successful investors what they did and how they got there. I have always found that experts in all walks of life are often willing to help out and offer advice where possible. Never be afraid to ask. Free advice is valuable as long as it comes from the right (experienced) source.

# 4. (Dad's) Multi Cultural Upbringing

Being able to come in from school at three in the afternoon, drop my clothes on the floor and have them washed and ironed and back in the wardrobe the next AM opened my eyes to a new world. With servants on hand, on demand food was available at any time of the day, and duties such as carrying my shoes and schoolbag to the school bus, which would arrive at the gate of our house every AM, made me want more of it. I'm not sure this way of life was useful to me later, as when I got back to reality and the first winter term at a British boarding school I got a sudden and shocking jolt.

I had seen how easy and how hard life can be to the extremes. Coming back to a British public school having grown up in a different expatriate culture made me an instant and easy target for the other kids to abuse at will.

Life became very hard for the first six months and I had to work to understand another way of life quickly. I have lived in so many different cultures and with so many different types of people; rich, poor, shop floor, chairman of the board, through all of my travels, and although it brought its challenges, I'm very thankful to my parents for giving me this start in life.

With Indonesia being a developing country, luxury car tax was in force, making a BMW or Mercedes 3 times the price of the same car in the UK. This made my desire to own BMW's, Mercedes and Porsche's much stronger than they would have I were in the UK. I spent a lot of my youth eulogising over relatively small engined 6 cylinder BMWs that would take CEOs to work in Jakarta. My appetite only grew when I returned to the UK and saw the cars I couldn't have come and pick the other kids up. Although at boarding school this was on a completely different scale with many parents arriving in Aston Martins, Ferraris, BMW M5s and S Class Mercedes. My father was on a much lower level in the car spectrum and if I'm honest I felt inferior. My mind was set in these years that at almost all cost I would have the means to buy the cars and huge houses that the parents of my classmates had. I already knew how to save and reduce cost as Dad had drilled me into this mindset. I just needed help with the making the money part. I could see that almost all of the money these super-rich parents had that their kids, my friends, were enjoying, was through business or property. Many of my friends were in line to inherit either huge lumps of cash or the business and properties that churned out the huge lumps of cash. It became crystal clear that I needed to own my own business and I became hell bent in these early years on doing this one day. I had a good cost cutting culture and a ready made network to start, I just missed a few of the vital pieces to complete the puzzle; I didn't have the high life and luxury I so desired.

## Lessons from my Dad

As a reward, every few months we'd return to the Intercontinental Hotel for Sunday brunch in Jakarta; an all you can eat affair of epic proportions. The best ingredients and chefs from around the world would make amazing food. Dad was a dichotomy; he would spend money on the best but scrimp on the mediocre (some of this has rubbed off I hasten to admit). I will spend money on eating at the best restaurants in the world (usually in London as I believe that most of them are there) but will rarely buy clothes unless they are in a sale. Mid week for a normal dinner for Gemma and I, I will want to use a voucher at Pizza Express which usually brings the dinner down to under £25, we will then walk outside and drive home in the Ferrari. I get a weird, somewhat rebellious pleasure in this.

Dad would however insist on the family being starved the day before, and absolutely on the morning of the brunch, to ensure maximum value was extracted from the sitting. Clearly he'd decided that good savings were to be made in the housekeeping budget to off-set the cost of the Borobudur Intercontinental Sunday Brunch. It was guaranteed on this occasion that my Dad would eat himself into a painful stupor, and Mum would exclaim 'your father's done it again.' The next 3 days he'd complain of chronic indigestion, yet with a strange sense of pride that he'd pushed the value to the maximum level. It reminds me when he went to a balti-hut with my Uncle on a trip back to Birmingham. Believing life was best experienced as a series of extreme events, he ordered a phaal balti, several times hotter than a Vindaloo, much to the amusement of my uncle and the waiting staff. 'I've lived all over the world and some balti in Birmingham won't get the better of me,' he stated publicly. After a few mouthfuls it became apparent that his demeanour was changing. Refusing to let paid for food go to waste, he continued to wade sweatily through the dish until every last bit of sauce had been polished by the naan, but this had a significant affect on his brain. He became aggressive to the waiting staff, causing a huge scene through chili-intoxication. A great story for me to hear afterwards and very funny as I wasn't there. In my younger years it would have got embarrassing (as I got older it moved to a form of entertainment for me).

*(NOW) I think my attitude to life formed from watching my Dad is certainly about creating experiences from which we create memories. Perhaps not as extreme or painful as my Dad loved, but important all the same. I do love paying for the best of something; an amazing hotel room, holiday, restaurant or experience, but I will stay there often just once or for short period of time, as the benefit starts to diminish as the reality kicks in. Clearly as I have become more successful things like that have become more normal and*

*the cost doesn't affect me much, so these tendencies have become more focused on to bigger items. It's like I am playing a constant second guessing game with myself to enjoy my life a little more than my Dad did but never taking it for granted, letting it become too normal, or over spending thus reducing the cost/benefit ratio.*

## Procedures

Dad was obsessed with procedures, and not just at work. Every Sunday AM, before we could go out as a family for the day, Dad would spend 2 hours walking around the house with the 'House-boy,' performing a full inspection (with check sheets) of every crevice of the house with a list of the previous weeks maintenance items which he would check off, or demand it be done to a higher standard. This military operation would create a mountain of painting, floor/trim repositioning, pool and window cleaning, taking scuff marks off surfaces, re-wiring electrical insulations and cutting the full 1.5 acre lawn with hand shears (because a lawn mower was too expensive). No joke. Once a fortnight this procedure of cutting elephant grass in a 2 acre garden was benchmark minimum. The poor Houseboy would have a months worth or work to do in a week, and get paid £8 a week for his efforts.

*[NOW] From this obsessive behaviour I learned that people need to be held accountable and checked upon frequently. If people don't have a gentle sense that they are being watched, measured or have specific goals and criteria to meet, then it is likely that the work will not be done, or it will be done their way. These checks give the opportunity for on the job training and for people to better understand the quality of work required.*

*Managing people, I believe, is much more effective with frequent (sometimes random) checks and measures, but people need to be given the correct tools to do the job (i.e. a lawnmower) and free reign to perform tasks in their own way and without constant micro-management.*

*The problem with being obsessively-compulsive about control and perfection is you expend way too much time and energy (and cost) controlling things which draw you away from your important tasks, goals and vision. There is a diminishing value of time where too much control, research, analysis or management actually gives negative benefit, and you need to know when to let go. Be careful not to go so deep into cost saving you create a low life quality. And believe me, I've juggled with this over the years, sometimes getting stuck in micro tasks that bring virtually no benefit.*

Dad was obsessively controlling over possessions. He had one each of the best pen-knife, top end watch, the best cigar in the world, the best lighter, the best suit, all fastidiously laid out in his top drawer, never to be used. They were equally spaced apart, and kept in mint condition with no fingermarks. He would often open his top drawer, stare at them for a while, and then shut it again.

One day he returned from work and for some reason I decided to tell him that I had seen his cigar tube in his top draw and taken a look at the cigar inside. I remember his face vividly; it changed to one of serious concern and when he ascertained that I had unscrewed the cap he went hopping mad. Unbeknownst to me, by unscrewing the cap I had let air into the tube which dramatically shortens the life of the cigar in its best smoke-able state. His cigar was ruined in his mind. He spent the next hour dancing around like a mad man (I think because he had lost control of something). I felt bad but didn't really know why or what I'd done.

Possessions are not worth this kind of upset and I made a decision to lord experiences over things I can own a long while ago. Memories and events hold more value than transient possessions. Dad used to get so mad over his prized (but never used) possessions, and for no good reason in my opinion as it made his life very stressful. Memories are the things you get to keep and that really mean something if you have done them with someone you care about.

*[NOW] Being brought up in this way, not only was I drilled into delaying gratification, I was drilled to never have any at all! My Dad died at 63, not getting much of the tangible benefit of all of his gratification-delaying tactics. I have since learned that although delaying gratification is a vital part of an effective investment and wealth strategy, there should be a certain amount of 'living for today.' It is, however, important to spend/invest only in those things that make you the happiest, because most of the depreciating assets that people spend so much money on gives them no immediate benefit, often leading to guilt and delayed or prolonged unhappiness.*

*You should spend time discovering (at low cost) what makes you the happiest in life, and as long as you never spend more than you earn, or you can buy an investment that will pay for it, enjoy your life while you are here. 80 years is not a long time and living for now is also important. My Dad's extreme obsession taught me that investing/saving can also go too far the other way.*

Dad died early from cancer at 63. He suffered for about 3 years with various forms which I suspect was linked amongst other things to the stress he created in his life. He was also a 3-5 a day smoker which didn't help and ate too much red meat. I don't smoke, I exercise 3-4 days a week and eat as much fruit and vegetables as I can as a result. I'm not a believer in much of the "latest" or new research/techniques in healthy eating/diets as I find the advice changes too much to make it credible. I'm convinced however that a simple strategy of low meat and fat diet high in fruit and vegetables will endure the test of time as a diet which keeps you healthy into old age. Reducing stress levels and having emotional consistency is also in my opinion key to this which is why I try and exclude people who lead me in another direction from my life. Dad lived with too much stress in my opinion, much of which was a self inflicted and could have been avoided.

## Summary

Investing today for a more rewarding tomorrow is what makes our lives so enjoyable and fulfilling. The key is to enjoy life living every phase as much as possible but there is a sweet spot, for investing and saving now for the future but yet living a quality life today. Balance saving with spending. To me, education is an investment. So is travel, as you are able to invest quality time with your loved ones. There are a lot of people with the money but not the time. If you are able to make time for yourself, then you are truly independent. If you can learn to tame greed and make big decisions to control your own emotions, you can also make some sound investment decisions. Enjoy life. Invest for your future.

# 5. The Contrast of Luxury

At 12 years old, I was sent back to England to start at a British boarding school. Having become used to the gentle regime of the British International School in Jakarta, I was thrust into a seriously hard regime in Oakham. Arriving fresh off the plane with my Sandals on and ex-pat language and culture, I became an instant and easy target for the other boys who were already acclimatised to the British way.

It was shocking to have to make my own bed, polish my shoes and conform to a strict routine with severe punishment for transgressions. I spent seven days a week in school uniform, including attending chapel 3 days a week. This was my first experience of real discipline, which my Dad thought was brilliant; 'exactly what you need to get on in the world.' My Mum wanted me home because for the first 6 months I was on the phone three times a week crying my eyes out to her. I found it so hard to integrate into this new world. The language, dress and attitudes of my peers at school were so alien to the extent that the only kids who would be friends with me were known as 'the losers.' Fine so I was enclosed into this little world with the geeks, but I wanted to be a winner. Slowly I managed to become 'cool' and gain the respect of the winners (kissing a few frogs along the way). This was probably my first experience of changing who I was very quickly, which I could use to my advantage in different social and business situations in the future. I know lots will think that I should have perhaps been more of an individual and fought change, but I knew I needed to align with the right people and learn a new culture to get on and ahead. Because I'd had so many cultural experiences I could adapt quickly to the network or environment.

The boarding house was like living in one of Dad's creations. It hadn't been renovated since the 70's with cold floors and a military installation feel. I found the lack of basic comforts tough, however when I went

A picture of William at work a few years ago

My Mum and William in Singapore in the 1990s.

home it really made me appreciate the finer things in life (carpet when we had it), being able to shower on your own, regulate the temperature yourself, and not with 8 other boys throwing things at you.

*[NOW] This probably formed my current view of luxury. Luxury is great as long as it is enjoyed with grounding and contrast. I certainly had a shielded view of luxury in the Far East, and had no concept of gratitude or polarity. Luxury means nothing if not contrasted with time without it or pining for it. To really value the luxury, saving or investing long enough to purchase it with the dividend, or as a reward for hard work or delayed gratification, is the best means to create gratitude and sustained happiness.*

*For me, all life is about contrast. Happiness and gratitude significantly increase, (as does the scale and sustainability of your business of investment portfolio) when you endure both luxury and delayed gratification. As a result, I intentionally like to experience cheap products, services and experience to assess and appreciate luxury that I might strive for. People often dream of luxury, but the reality is a often a let down. This is not just because of the dream, but because they never really created the contrast properly. You should also get very clear on what you truly value in life, so that you can have the great experiences you pine for.*

*For example, when I went to University I purchased my £46 brown 1984 Vauxhall Nova from the auction. The auction fee was £16 and the car was £30. When I bought it, it had around 120,000 miles on the clock, and I drove it onto the ground for 3 years through University, putting another 55,000 miles on the clock. My Dad drilled me on doing maintenance myself, I conducted an oil and filter change every 3,000 miles as Dad said the engine would then last forever. The filter was £1.84 and oil was £2.79 for 5L, which I bought from Millfield Autos in Peterborough.*

*This got me off the bus, and into a vehicle my Dad was proud of. I'd already saved around £15,000 at 19, making these key purchasing decisions that allowed me to save so much money. My peers at University either had money given to them by their parents or were taking out student loans and overdrafts. This gave me a real sense of achievement and satisfaction.*

*When Rob and I picked up our first Ferrari, it was an unbelievable experience to drive home in this car. It was a surreal and almost unreal experience. This gave me a real and memorable experience of excitement, and driving home with the louder than a fog horn exhaust and the feeling of the wind on my face with the roof down was truly electrifying. This experience was as much created by driving a 19 year old car for 3 years at University as it was a £140,000 Ferrari (which we purchased for £68,500 at the near-bottom of the depreciation curve).*

The whole process of changing from a life of relative luxury in the sun with servants abroad, to the realities of a cold winter at a Boarding School wasn't helped by the fact that my Mum decided to separate and divorce my Dad. They hadn't been happy for many years and Mum knew her opportunity was when we were back in the UK and I was settled in at school.

They both found new partners and I was lucky in that I got a new step Dad , William. He cares a lot about my Mum and looks after her really well, I had (and still do have) a great relationship with him - he has helped me understand many systems and procedures in property and supported my Entrepreneurial endeavours. He enjoyed looking at new business ideas with me, enthusing and encouraging me to do things which helped me to develop. Many of the basic systems that he helped me to develop are still used in our property buying process today. They keep the person buying the deals to a set format and ensure that refurbishment costs don't spiral. It was this grounding that helped me to replicate this across other business functions and create software such as the deal analyser, refurb costings system, BOQ's (Bill of Quantity) and HMO evaluation sheets. This knowledge then grew into a system to manage client purchases from end to end; bespoke property management software developed by an external consultant. This system has helped us immeasurably.

In hindsight Mum did exactly the right thing, she got someone who she could rely on to care for her and treat us all well and she became much happier for it.

## Summary

Buying luxury items should be done with passive income. Unfortunately, too many people make the mistake of buying luxury with their earned incomes. I see it all the time. Worse, some go into debt for the luxuries. All these items eat away at investment capital that should be better put to use. When you spend earned income on luxury items, you damage your finances. Earned income should go into one of three buckets; living, saving and investing. The two steps to achieve before you buy a luxury item is, build up a "war chest" by reserving cash, then begin investing diligently. Not only is this rewarding and leads to less regret, your earned income will cover your monthly expenses, your war chest will still be available and your investments haven't lost their principle value. You no longer have to steal from any of the three buckets to live a life of luxury.

# 6. Moving into the (cheeky) world of business

At 13, I started to form friendships in England, and would often go round to my friend Sam's house where I met his father, Ken. He is a tough, towering figure, who has spent the last 35 years running a medium-sized business and building wealth. Ken is no nonsense; definitely a saver rather than a spender, with a distinct hatred of debt. When Sam was 13, Ken had Sam selling products for him to friends at school and providing services such as furniture removals and wedding care hire. This was my first taste of business, which didn't come out of a textbook.

My Dad admired business people but never was one, and didn't understand business very deeply. I'd watch Ken with his huge house, Merc S-class, three kids at boarding school, and enough cash in his pocket to sink a battleship, and wonder how he did it. I wanted a big piece of this.

Through our teens, Sam became more and more involved in importing products and wholesaling them to market traders. I got first hand experience at the coalface of negotiations and deals in my teens. Most of the other kids were interested in spending money on music, sports and going out and impressing girls. I wasn't bothered about any of that, I just wanted to make money, so dealing and trading at 15 was very exciting to me and gave me real world insights into how to make money, rather than what you watched on TV.

Ken would always encourage us whilst on holiday to do a bit of business while we were abroad, bringing goods back which we could sell to 'pay for our airfare.'

*[Now] Joint appreciation of the low cost high life school of thought is shared by another friend of mine; Adrian. Since my mid teens we have shared and*

*developed much theory getting maximum luxury living and highest bang for the buck, for which I'm most grateful. Spending time with people who are well versed in the areas you want to focus compounds the success and keeps your fire burning.*

In the late 90's the Euro was very weak, and we could get Cars within the common market, at up to 25% cheaper than from UK dealers. Manufactures were forced to sell cars to exactly the same spec as the UK models, in the EU at the rate for that currency, and could not discriminate against foreigners from within the EU. We spotted this weak Euro as an opportunity to buy Cars very cheaply, and import them to the UK.

I would scour the manufacturer directories for dealers in three or four countries that I knew had cheap supply. I would then fax every single one asking them to provide a price for a UK spec car for import to the UK, free of VAT and local taxes. After a few weeks of research and negotiations, I'd place an order, ensuring that they provide a European certificate of conformity along with the necessary paperwork to register the car in the UK, whilst keeping the Inland Revenue happy. We'd then fly to over Ireland or mainland Europe for collection.

Even though we were mature in business relative to our other 17 year old peers at school, we were still 17 year-old kids. We'd see this as a holiday-cum-business trip, and any excuse for frivolity was never declined. One trip, after getting off the Ferry,

Sam turned the return leg with the cars as a Gumball rally style challenge through the Pennines. On this trip we had 2 brand new, yellow, turbo-charged Fiat Punto GT's, which retailed at £15K in the UK, that we'd paid £9K for, though both needed a new set of tyres once we got back home! I was able to source them cheaply, of course.

Once we returned with the cars, still warm and ticking, we'd advertise them in Auto trader. We'd own them all summer, cruising or thrashing them around town, feeling great. My friends at school could not get their heads around how we had such great Cars. At the end of the summer we'd sell them at a profit with 3,000 on the clock; an easy grand a car. A lot of money back then and at that age.

I would *always* save all the money I made.

*[NOW] I gained valuable lessons in research through importing the Cars which I still carry with me today. Here are some of them:*

# Research

*The research involved going into Car supermarkets and actually seeing the Cars they had advertised with big discounts that were imported (this is very important and I'm gob smacked how many people think 'desktop valuations,' of any investment actually stack up). I'd get hold of the service book (sometimes they were in the Car or I'd have to persuade the receptionist to show me the manual where the service book was located). I'd look for information on who the supplying dealer was by checking the pre delivery inspection stamp in the service book, and therefore finding the source of the dealers and which EU dealers were exporting cars on the cheap. It is really important to actually see, or have in your hands, the proof of the certificates or whatever other verification or warranty process you are researching. It's not real until it's in your hand just like you don't have money until it's in the bank.*

Not only is it important to do your research, but often you have to be a little *cheeky* to get the *real information*, or the source behind the source. *I was never afraid to sniff around, spy on competitors and use a couple of* smiles and tricks that Sam and Ken taught me to get the deep, often hidden, but most important information that others would miss or keep from you. To this day I still use the same strategies to research buying in any investment class. Sam & Ken can both turn on the charm and I picked up on this useful technique.

Apart from having the cash, the main barrier to having Cars like that at our age was the insurance. Of course it is even worse now. I learned that the assumptions of others that Cars like that were uninsurable to under 21's (or at a cost of over £2,000) could be overcome with extensive research. I'd ring 20 insurance companies, quickly learning who the route underwriters were, so I could gain an understanding of which ones viewed young drivers in high performance cars in a less bad light, and were pricing accordingly. This is a valuable trait, as most people give up after a handful of tries resigning to defeat, but the answer or best solution is often a few layers deeper. Sure, it may be a little harder to find, but that means it is harder for everyone else too, so the competition there is much less. Remember when it is hard for you it's hard for them too, and I get satisfaction and motivation in that. When we bought our first Ferrari, I called scores of insurance companies, and because I was in my 20's, I got lots of rejection, finally finding a quote of £5,000. A couple of layers down was a specialist insurer who insured us at £800. A cool £4,200 to save, compound and invest for 50 years plus, and an 84% discount no less!

This taught me to both enjoy research, and use it as my competitive advantage. Most people I know don't value this 'digging' in the same way, or give up before they get deep enough to gain an advantage. There is nearly always a way to get a cheaper flight, cheaper insurance quote, better understanding of real value, getting a property valued correctly, buying an asset cheaply, all in how deep you dig and the more seriously you take research. I'm not talking about the surfing the 'net type, I'm talking about

A picture of the 2 BMW M3's Sam I and bought to keep and sell on in our early 20's. Self earned and invested in. We actually bought them in the UK but had them on order for 2 years prior to delivery as we expected them to be worth more nearly new as there was always a big waiting list on these Cars.

the aggressive, thorough digging into how a system really works. You get to the route of the knowledge and it gives you a competitive advantage. You cut through noise, fluff, and people's inaccurate assessments of their reality

## Market variances

In importing Cars, I learned the importance of switching your strategy to one that works in the current, existing and or local market. The strategy to import Cars profitably *was totally reliant on a weak Euro back when we were doing it. This lasted for a specific (short) window, which I took advantage of, but once the Euro strengthened, it all ended. Manufactures also cottoned on, and found ways of restricting it through back door disciplining of dealers and reduced warranties on imported Cars. I find this is how business works. Business evolves and your strategy must be flexible to adapt, or you die. As Ray Croc of McDonalds says: 'If you're green you grow, if you're red you rot.' There are cycles and micro cycles, and you have to re-evaluate and refocus your business direction and energy into the direction in which a market is behaving. Again, this means change when you are secure, and this can be unsettling, but it is for everyone else too, so your competition reduces to the same degree of the nature and extremity of the change. The recent recession showed this; it was very tough for many but fertile ground for huge growth for the Contrarians.*

## If it's too good to be true...

In 2000, the stock market, tech industries, Nasdaq (and media) boom was going crazy. I saw this as a big opportunity. I was reading all the financial press, getting really excited and investing all my student loans like the stock market was about to close tomorrow. I found through the FT that by signing up to an internet service provider called 'Totalise,' I could get gifted about £500 worth of free shares. To me this was £500 for nothing, and I thought that £500 today was going to be £50,000 in a few short years. I got all my friends involved so that they could benefit and get free shares too, and we'd all make £1,000's.

Some of my friends signed up and cashed the shares straight away, and one went out and bought a hi-fi separates system. I tried to persuade them keep the shares and re-invest them. Why would you want to cash out when they could be £10,000's in a few months? In hindsight, selling immediately proved to be a (the only) wise decision.

I invested my student loans ('free' money) into Jellyworks, which were 5p in the AM and by close of the market they'd hit a quid. That was a 20 fold increase in 1 day. I kept doing my spreadsheets, compounding it all up, and could see a vision of a guaranteed route to millions. I further invested into Stepstone Human Resources and all these companies/ stocks (with a common thread that they all had little or no track record, no profitability and had been valued so highly based on the having 'internet' or 'technology' in their name, that they came with a 'guaranteed' success certificate). Predictably, and with hindsight and experience, the market began to unwind and unravel into a huge crash, taking with it about £10,000 of my student loans. Rob tells me how he 'pissed his away' at University, and I can't say that this was much different to be frank. Though I learned valuable lessons.

I had been buying 'assets' based on expected future capital growth rather than the current income or dividend that the asset produces. I had bought based on *other people's* expectation of future growth such as journalists, and got caught up in the hype and frenzy; something you need to be able to control and take a step back from. For a start most journos know/knew very little about these markets, and secondly nobody can predict when any capital growth will come. You can often predict roughly what will happen with an investment, just not when. I certainly treat property purchases this way now. I will always focus on the income or immediate guaranteed forced capital growth through buying cheap or converting rather than general capital growth where the timing and amount is not predictable.

***[NOW] The (hard lessons) I had to learn were:***

1.   *Don't invest in anything I don't understand*

2.   *If investing in the stock market, only invest for the long term*

3.   Only invest in real companies which have a proven track record and profitability

4.   Only invest in companies that sell real products and services that I can relate to and <u>verify</u>

5.   Diversify investments into uncorrelated assets

6.   High returns equal higher risk

7.   If £500 of shares are being given away for free, perhaps ask yourself why you shouldn't sell quickly!

8.   Don't invest based on what (non specialised, ulterior motived, non experienced) journalists advise

9.   Don't be pulled along by the hubris of the market

10.  If everyone else is doing it, it probably means it is bad

I felt very embarrassed about losing all this money. I wanted to feel like my peers respected me and felt that I knew what I was doing, and the fact that I'd lost all that money showed that I didn't. I also managed to persuade MBNA to give me a £15K limit, and was in the throws of opening a spread betting account, which would have enabled me to multiply my 'winnings' (or losses in this case) by five. Thank God it all imploded before my testicles got big enough to dump it all in. Forgive me for the repeated reference.

After these big lessons I still managed to retain around £5K in savings, and since that day have always ensured I have many layers of protection money and 'capital preservation,' to ensure my wealth is robust. I explain this in detail later.

# Blockbusting

At University, I dusted myself down and started up a DVD rental business. I found a cheap supplier in Thailand using the same research strategies I'd learned buying Cars. If we were ever on holiday anywhere, Sam would want to go to the local markets and find the wholesalers supplying them and set up a supply line back to the UK. I created a supply line of DVD's back to the UK, where they would post them to me at a highly discounted per unit cost. I would rent these DVD's out to people in the student union, offering a home delivery service in my Nova. I would get hold of releases often earlier than others could obtain them in the UK, which was very attractive to my peers. Once I got into the halls, I'd upsell other products; nachos, drink, cigarettes etc. Because I had a captive audience they'd pay over the rate they could purchase in the local supermarket, for the convenience. I didn't know anyone else at the University who was doing this. I slapped posters up across all the halls of residences, much to some sociology lecturer's dismay, and I'd get frequent calls for business (and the odd call from a lecturer). I think they thought I was a bit strange, as the normal thing to do was to go and get a bar job, but I felt like I was learning essential business and Entrepreneurial skills that I could leverage and monetise in the future. I probably managed to stash away £10,000 from this business, which of course I saved. This was the equivalent of 3 years of student loans or 2 years working 4 shifts a week in a bar (or a week in Jellyworks!). I had also done it without needing to listen to a boss or someone I didn't like.

*[NOW] The key lessons I got from my halls of residence DVD rental business are:*

- *Test at low risk your product range tirelessly until you find what your customers want*

- *You need to be providing a unique selling proposition, something that others don't have so that you can keep your prices at a good level and make margin*

- *Don't be afraid of competition, it probably just means there is a good market*

- *Don't listen to others who are negative about your business or likelihood of success, in fact cast them adrift and find new friends*

- *Don't be afraid to push the boundaries. Some of the products I imported were grey imports which the manufacturer had intended for other markets. By selling them myself it probably didn't make them happy, but you need to push the boundaries in the early days to get started*

## 1. Selling

*Selling is something that I could do as long as I could get enthused about something and transfer that to others. So many people have fears and hang ups about selling. I guess I was lucky in that it was something I just knew you had to do, and never really had any issues or fears doing it. I could easily point out benefits, and even increase emotional desire through social proof and scarcity; laws which are vital in todays world if you want to get ahead. Although the right product and the right margin were of more interest to me, selling is a must have skill for any Entrepreneur, investor or businessperson. You simply have to embrace it or you don't grow your business. Find something you're passionate about and it's easy.*

## 2. Customer service

*I discovered that the easier I made it for the customer to buy, the more I sold. I focused on offering an immediate, fast service, and the home delivery to the students was a great benefit to them (especially as most of them were really lazy). I thought it was important to be reliable and always turn up when you said you would, giving them what they wanted. If I spotted good customers out in the student union, I'd always buy them a drink; the investment would go a long way, and something I remember from my Dad schmoozing up the local traffic Police.*

*Without your customers, you have no business. Focus on giving them a unique service and high perceived value. Focus on them as much as you do your margins, and they will become your best sales team. Remember that everything you do by them is being judged, and you're being recommended or you're not. If you're not you have to spend to find new customers, and this has diminishing returns, especially in mature markets. When you start and you're small and lean, this is a definite advantage over the bigger, more sluggish competitors have several layers of org chart, board members and red tape to make any decision. Like deeper levels of research, use this to your advantage.*

## 3. Getting products/stock that sold and people wanted

*I worked out how to do 'customers surveys' and 'market research,' very early, cheaply, and with low risk. I would constantly ask my customers what DVD's they wanted, and worked out what was renting best. I would adjust my stock not according to what I wanted or loved, but according to what was demanded by my customers. I would offer them cheaper prices if they introduced me to their mates.*

*Too many people when starting a business do what they love, trying to make it fit as a business. They set up a cake shop because they love cakes, or a restaurant because they love cooking, but actually have no idea if the model will work, if the area has demand, if there is enough footfall and so on. I learned that you should find out what is proven to work, and has deep demand, and sell this. I guess I was lucky because my passion wasn't a particular product, service or niche, it was (and still is) business itself. Keep your passion for business, and don't get too attached to your products. Start small, start now, test first, upscale later.*

### 4. Upselling, cross selling & downselling

*Students who watched DVD's also wanted Fags, Doritos and other products. I would find complimentary products that went with their DVD's, and then upsell them at point of sale while they were 'captive.' It worked best when they were just handing over the cash, as they were already in a buying mindset, and a few extra products were an easy decision with the money already out. This strategy would often double my evening's take home.*

*Companies like Amazon have mastered this and created a huge global retail empire with fast, easy and relevant upselling at point of sale. This lesson has helped Progressive make many £millions more in sales. In business, the hardest thing is getting the credit card out of the wallet (engaging the buying decision), so once they have decided to buy, a little addition at point of sale is usually easy, but an opportunity most business miss. Would you like to buy any of our other books?!*

*Upselling is offering another product at a higher value or level, or an add on (such as a new strap for a watch or warranty for a car), cross selling is selling across at a similar or alternative level (insurance companies selling gadget insurance with home or car insurance) and down selling is offering a cheaper alternative if your customer doesn't buy (online training or DVD's instead of the live event).*

## Electronic auctions

I spotted an early opportunity to get into the new market of selling products as your own retailer, or e-seller. I felt this was a huge market, because of the ease at which you could sell things, and the convenience at which the end user could buy. I joined a free auction site for selling goods direct to consumer, called QXL. I was selling clothing and other in-fashion consumer items that I was importing from Thailand and China. The margins on this strategy were in the 100's of percentage points, and there was virtually no overhead. Business was changing fast and retailers with stock and premises and overhead were hurting and little start ups like me were disrupting the old way of doing things.

*[NOW] The revelation in this to me was 'marketing.' Marketing was never naturally my strong point, and I didn't know how to 'attract' or buy customers on a very large scale. The beauty of QXL was that not only was it an engine to sell goods C2C, it was a marketing platform that pulled in a large volume of customers right to your e-door. I recall this being my first experience of understanding what marketing was all about, and no business can survive without (good) marketing. If you own a shop and a great shop assistant is the 'sales' then getting people in the door is the 'marketing.'*

*I also had a turning point about the difference between 'free' and 'value.' The huge volume of traffic and sales on QXL made it so worth the very small cost to list the item (open my e-shop door), and multiplied the amount of money I could make several times over. This is something my Dad may not have had the chance to find out, but often you have to spend some money to make some money. Before then I was, like my Dad, a complete tight-arse about every single cost; often leaving the big profits on the table for someone else. Marketing is one of your best investments in your business, and investments need funding. Marketing is a spend that should not be sacrificed, and often the thing that businesses cut back on in recessions.*

## My Degree

At this point it has just dawned on me that we haven't even talked about my degree. I studied International Business Economics at UWE Bristol. I always wanted to study business or economics, both from natural interest and imposed on me by my Dad, who was ecstatic about my enrolment. I quite enjoyed juggling a few sideline businesses whilst 'studying,' as both were part of a greater vision I had to be in business and be an investor. Also, I didn't really gel with many of the other students on my course. I wanted to make money, and would spend all my Sunday's dreaming up business ideas, but they would go drinking on a Sunday afternoon down the local. I wasn't really into the whole boozing behaviour. Although into it when I was younger, I prefer to get to bed early and dream up money making ideas and Entrepreneurial endeavours.

I suppose I'm pretty right wing if I'm honest, which made my first year at University even more interesting as I was living with a bunch of self-righteous sociology students who believed that I was the devil because I wanted to be in business and make money. They'd come in every night intoxicated with their socialist workers party rhetoric, clutching the Guardian, ranting about how their family's situation was inferior because of bastard businessmen (like me). This was the late 90's version of banker bashing, and my futile attempts to try and persuade them to be enterprising, go into business and drag themselves out of their victim situation was met with drunken, aggressive abuse. They would chant Marxist slogans to me, the Anti-Christ, while reading their twisted sociology textbooks that taught them that the only reason Russian and Chinese communism had failed was because it wasn't 'real communism,' or as Karl Marx had intended. They refused to accept my point that Marx's idealistic model probably hadn't been adopted in totality because it wasn't workable or practical in the real world. Incentive is the key to any successful society.

So needless to say, the sociology module of my degree was an opportunity for me to sit there and disagree with the lefty lecturers. It didn't last very long as I simply stopped attending this module. I learned not to focus my energy and valuable time into those who had another ideal or vision; it only creates animosity and distracts you from your grand vision. Smile, tip your cap and go and change the world in your own way. I must admit to wasting a lot of energy here with people I was never going to change.

I do believe that there are a lot of people who adopt a victim/the world has dealt me a bad card mentality. If they switched this energy to taking responsibility for themselves and developing a business or career which would earn the money to get out of this situation, they would probably become successful over time. You can make excuses or you can make money, you can't make excuses and money.

## Summary

**Pick out people whose behaviour is better than yours and you'll drift in those directions in your thirst** for *learning and improvement*. Only play the game when you have ensured your chances of losing are slim. Understanding a business really well can help you smell trouble from miles away. Also, you can never have conviction in something you do not understand, and *conviction* is what enables you to pounce on an opportunity when the time is right. Practice emotional discipline and take your investing to the next level.

# 7. Economics & the real world of the addicted Entrepreneur

Some of the most valuable lessons I learned were in my macro-economic lectures, where we were taught about the power of interest rates, inflation, economic growth, currency movements, supply and demand curves, the money supply and monetary and fiscal policy. My grounding in interest rate policy and inflation were the building blocks to creating the property portfolio I have now. Supply and demand curves still shape my investment strategy today, and the economics of business are relevant in the pricing strategies both in business and investing. I was particularly interested in absorbing this content because it was delivered by a complete Don of economics, John Sloman, who advised the government on economic policy and wrote the book that many economics students read today.

*[NOW] It is very important to assess the source of your knowledge. Too many people have an opinion on anything and everything they know nothing about. I really respected John Sloman for what he had done, who he advised and what he knew. I now only take business and investing advice or make key decisions based on the knowledge I gain from people who have done it, and are great at it. A lot of people talk a good game, but can they play it? Find the people with the best knowledge and take advice from them, politely (or otherwise) ignoring the rest. Everyone in the UK seems to think they know about property and being an Entrepreneur. But do they? Have the editors of the tabloids built a significant cash flowing portfolio? In case you're in any doubt, I know many of them, and I can tell you they don't. Some famous ones too who have a surprisingly small amount of property. You simply must be discerning in who you take advice from, what you read and which programmes you watch on TV.*

This is by no means an economics textbook, but many of the above modules will rear their head throughout the rest of the book.

# The Entrepreneurial addiction

By the end of University I had, or was involved in, around a dozen businesses or investment classes. I felt this gave me good experience at my age; a good nose for the types of businesses or investments that really work, an understanding of risk, how to spot opportunities and start businesses, and I had a few quid in my pocket that I'd created myself, with no help or hand-me-downs. I was proud of this, and believe you will gain much humble pride and self worth for starting, creating and building something yourself that matters and makes a difference.

And then I went and got a job!

Once I had finished University, my Dad saw it as the only next course of action to go on a management training scheme. He was all about training as he'd run training divisions for overseas development projects for governments and companies for 20 years. On a management training scheme you get to go in every department of a business and get practical training in the right way (in his view) with low risk.

In the 3$^{rd}$ year of University I applied for about 20 management training placements. I quickly worked out that you could have influence over your predicted grades, as by the time you got your job offer out, you already had your results. A 2:1 seemed appropriate to fill in on the applications, and I got accepted onto an Irish meat company, ABP, management training scheme.

# The real world

ABP was the real world. This was my first (real) job. My first 'job' previously was at a major fast food chain; I was on 'chips and times.'

This consisted of chips, chicken dippers, hot wings, hash browns – making sure they were topped up and 'in time.' It was a hard job and it taught me how hard some people have to work for not a lot of money (and how un-leveraged they were). This heightened my desire to make big money on my terms rather than stand on my feet all day sliding around on greasy floors cooking frozen chips and talking to drunk football fans. My boss' management style was to punch me when he wanted to show his authority, and the frequent dead legs also created a desire to control my own destiny and never have to work for anyone.

*(NOW) Some people really do work hard for their money, with rarely anything left after bills to spend or invest. Whether right or wrong, fair or otherwise, the smartest, wealthiest people I know work the least in terms of 'physical,' or practical labour, yet earn the most. Hard work in this day and age does not equal wealth, in fact it often equals the opposite. Many lower level roles and previous 'technical,' skills are being replaced by technology, machinery and even drones now. The world is moving faster than ever and people at the lower levels are becoming less relevant. Being creative, adaptable, lean, connected, leveraging other people's networks and expertise, and gaining the most knowledge in your field, whether fair or otherwise, makes you successful. I personally find these easier and more fun that manual labour anyway. Most people are working too hard to be rich and the Darwinian 'survival of the fittest,' is now 'survival of the most adaptable.'*

*But with this fast change comes great opportunity. You can literally start your business with a laptop and a Wi-Fi connection; virtually no overhead, online and instant access to millions of customers, free marketing on social media sites, easy set up of payment gateways and off the shelf websites, blogs to create die hard fans and a more level playing field with the super corporations.*

When I arrived at ABP, I was put in the buying office and spent my day buying and negotiating VL (trimmed meat that forms mince). I'd buy about 400 tonnes a week, supplying the whole of Asda's stock. I'd also do ad hoc tasks for the quality control manager and plant manager. The culture of the plant I worked at initially was young and fast paced; very much a trader environment. The guys in management were making good money in their early 30's, and we'd spend a lot of it in the local bar on Champagne on Friday and Saturday nights.

*(NOW) I learned early that staying 'in' with the right people in the company was paramount. Good contacts high up the org chart could propel you to higher jobs. One particular plant manager, in charge of a whole factory for the biggest meat supplier in Europe, gave me a great review to the operations director, and he in turn gave a series of good placements at different factories around the country. My Dad and the Policeman came instantly to mind.*

But while I was working for ABP, I was investing on the side in all the spare time I had. I'd started investing in property, and had bought a new build investment in Peterborough for £131,500, signed up for a flat in Bulgaria for 60,000 Euro plus furniture, and an off plan flat in Leicester.

Ironically, as we'll discuss later, the new build worked out well (even though I would have done much better if I had invested it in an existing/ older property). I flipped it when it was ready in 2004 making a small profit. The Bulgarian saga was quite different. I purchased a 1 bed flat for Euro 65,000 (or around £45,000 at the time) 'near' to the ski lift, in a new resort, feeling sure that big profits would follow. Following 8-12 visits to the notary public in the UK every time I wanted to get something done (at a cost of nearly £200 a rime), the flat was eventually built in 2007, more than 3 years on. Rob and I went skiing and I managed to rent it to a couple of other people for the next 4 years until I decided to sell it. After renting it for less than a month for the whole time I had owned it (and I week had been to Rob who didn't pay me!), it had cost me around £5k a year in mortgage, service charge and utilities just to own it! In 2011 I decided to sell and got £25,000 for it. This crystallised an overall loss of around £50,000 on a flat that cost £45,000!! That gives a whole new dimension/definition to 'negative equity.' This has to be one of my worst investments ever, but I got some valuable 'entrance fee' lessons I'll be revealing later at no extra cost to you.

So I'd caught the bug of property by watching Ken insist that Sam purchased a property when he was 18, live in it, and rent all the rooms out to cover the mortgage. Ken knew that a capital repayment mortgage was a form of forced savings. Sam, being wayward, spending lots and enjoying himself, could learn many valuable lessons in saving, investing, dealing with tenants and pulling rent in with a view to making profit over and above the mortgage payment. Ken 'loaned' Sam the money and Sam got to keep all income over the mortgage.

Ken, being a Wiley ol' dog, had also worked out that the market was about to go skitty in the mid to late '90's, as interest rates had dropped significantly and the country had firmly come out of recession. Ken put the deposit in, guaranteed the mortgage in Sam's name, and got Sam as early as he could into property. As long as the mortgage was covered, Sam kept the profit after costs. Not only this, but Ken bought a complete wreck for around £105,000, which Ken thought was a good price, and the entire family went in doing the full refurb: painting, clearing the garden, overseeing adding an extension, and in the next 2 years the price rocketed to over £160,000. This gave Sam a grounding of the reality of work and business and an 'enterprise' opportunity to create income.

As I watched Sam rent out the rooms to his mates in wonderment and make such a huge amount of money with a relative lack of knowledge and input, a switch went off in me that I could do this too, and make big money. But all I could hear in my ear was that a mortgage is a 'noose around your neck,' from guess who, preventing you from living overseas (which Dad wanted for me). Add to this that renting and dealing with tenants was a constant fight and all they did was wreck places; Dad's voices of doubt were that it was all such a huge risk. Interest rates could double like they did in the late 80's and you could lose everything.

*[Now] As I look back at what Ken did for Sam back then, it was totally inspired. It gave Sam his initial foundations and on the ground education, so that by his early 30's he probably had over £200,000 in real equity from that one deal, plus all the income. But more than that, it taught him the benefits of enterprise, how to pick tenants, how to get money in from tenants, property maintenance, some tough reality of dealing with people in business, and of course the benefits of making a profit and being rewarded for your effort and Entrepreneurialism. Sam also learned all the things you can do with that extra cash.*

*As soon as any children I have are 18, I will be doing exactly the same thing, getting them on the housing ladder with a mortgage that I guarantee. This is a far cry from just giving them a house, this is about assisting them in being a real property investor and business person through real life experience and opportunity, with gentle support and mentorship. Not that I am an expert in parenting, so please don't view this as parental advice!*

## Beg for forgiveness, don't ask for permission

*I later found out that the refurb the Burt's had done had no planning permission for the extension. I'd been told that this would cause 'huge problems,' when they came to sell the house, but Ken simply cracked on anyway and the sale went straight through no problem at all. This was my first major lesson in how many people worry so much about all the bad things that could happen, instead of focusing on solving issues that have actually become a problem, are a real problem, or are a commercial reality. The biggest risk of all is in not taking any, but how do you ever know what the 'boundaries' are unless you discover in reality what lies either side of them? Profit frequently comes from doing what others won't or can't because they are scared of what might happen, but in reality rarely does. Don't break the law, but find ways to gain advantage that others don't have the stomach for by testing the boundaries: 'beg for forgiveness, don't ask for permission.' If in doubt, test. Only the market will tell you what works and doesn't, so by all means get well educated, but then you've got to test it. I like to 'plan less and test more,' starting smaller the higher the risk.*

## My version of a Management Training Scheme

I stayed the two year course of management training at ABP, but chose to leave because I'd already started investing in property. I'd always wanted my own business, always wanted to be financially independent and I saw an opportunity to leave and get my own, Entrepreneurial version of 'management training.' I had a small portfolio while at work and wanted to be able to scale this more, and the time at ABP was taking me away from my main vision. I was grateful for what I learned.

The first ever buy to let property I bought, a new build in Hampton from Barratt Homes which I signed up for (off plan) in 2003, I got for £131,500. In the twelve months it took to build, the developer was selling them for £165,000. When I came to rent or sell it, I met a local Letting Agent who went beyond just Lettings; he was into investment. Des, the owner of the Agency, was someone who I respected, and as I got to know him he gave me a lot of insights into the rental market and the types of properties to buy and invest in. He was quite a rare breed, in that most Letting Agents have no knowledge of investing (many of them think they do), whereas he was an investor himself, and knew both markets very well. He became an unwitting local mentor. This was an early experience for me in the importance of having mentors (who have the specific knowledge you need).

As it transpired, I decided to sell the off plan new build I bought from Barratt, and I got £155,000 for it, but with the developer still able to sell the same property for substantially more, I got my first lesson in how new builds depreciate as soon as they are purchased, as does virtually anything purchased new. Most build properties devalue by about 10-15% as soon as you buy them. Like a new Car, they are no longer perfect once someone has lived in them, and depreciate in much the same way. This will happen even if they are indistinguishable from new. Once the developers marketing spend is gone, units like this are very hard to sell for the same price. The reality is that the market moves upwards over time, and this instant drop in price from new is masked by natural growth in the market. People will often sell their properties some years later and wonder why their new build went up less than an older house over the same period – this is why. Conversely, this masking of depreciation in growth gives apparent profit to speculators who confuse 'growth protection,' for skill, and they'll usually end up doing one new deal too many and get burned. This is exactly what happened to me; my first new build made profit through beginners luck and 'growth protection,' and my Bulgaria ski flat showed me the reality!

Once I'd built trust, Des showed me a better way of investing that was not common knowledge. To this point, all I really knew was to buy a property you needed a deposit and a mortgage, and to buy another property you needed another deposit and another mortgage. Although this would work in the long term, it was a frustratingly a slow process for me, not being flush with cash from an inheritance or lottery win. Des opened my eyes to innovative investing strategies including investing with little or no deposit, and investing with deposits but pulling them back out in quick succession (a model we've now refined and call the 'Buy, Refurb, Remortgage,' model, or BRR) so that I could buy many more properties quickly with less cash. I also learned that if you can find a good deal or someone with money 'buys into you,' you can partner with others and use their funds and your time/knowledge/sweat equity to 'joint venture' (JV).

I've been completely addicted to the concept of investing from an early age, and I found the concept of being able to buy unlimited amounts of property using a finite amount of funds totally intoxicating. It is an amazing gift, and I feel as passionate about this concept today as the time I discovered it. No other business I've ever seen gives you such leverage. But, you can push it too far, as I was about to find out.

## Summary

Addiction to investing certainly isn't a bad thing. In fact, I'm guilty of exhibiting this behaviour!. Such drive and risk-taking has led to big fortunes for investors and has also ruined the financial futures of many others. I've learned from looking back at my attitude towards investing that it is essential to building wealth but it is important not to be drowned in the moment or the 'Magpie syndrome;' chasing all that shines because it could be the next big thing. Investing in the property market or any business – the big pot of gold that it is – is a long term endeavour. Combine sound intellect with emotional discipline which leads to rational behaviour.

# 8. The Shortcut?

Des suggested that there was a shortcut to the 'Buy, Refurb, Remortgage,' model of putting deposits in, and remortgaging them out. He introduced me to another business of his, 'Property Dogs,' with his business partner who for the purposes of this book we will call Chris. For a fee payable to them, you could buy a property 'no money down.' Chris had various UK and overseas 'schemes,' which you could get into without 'deposits.'

When I first met Chris, I went into his office which he shared with Des and his Letting Agency, I was very surprised as he didn't fit my perceived notion of what a successful businessman would be like. He had an air of anger and brashness about him, constantly red-faced, shifting and fidgety and always had his hands in his pockets, fiddling and twitching. I found it strange yet what I thought he knew intrigued me so. Although my very first memories of meeting him are clouded, every person that I introduced him to got the same feeling: he was full of shit. You didn't know why at first, but you could smell the turd in every mannerism. He would force his opinions on you from the early minutes, which clearly lacked much understanding or foresight. He seemed to believe that the more you forced your opinions onto people, the more they would bend to your will.

Chris was ex military and ex transport police. He was like an overweight, bullied, failed sergeant major who had just stumbled upon something that he didn't understand, but got in at the right time. He described his property investing system as a 'remortgage cash machine.' And he'd say it like he was announcing numbers in a Bingo hall:

'The RE mortgage CASH MAAAAACHINE. Ohhhhhh YES!'

'Ohhhhh YES would end every sentence-cum-pitch and it was in the same accent as the nodding Churchill Dog. Chris would hide away in his office in-between his 37 daily espresso shots and consume himself with scams on the internet for most of the day staring at High Yielding Investment Programs (HYIPs) promising 50%+ PA returns, and e-gold trading and all sorts which I viewed as Ponzi schemes.

His favourite saying from those days was 'Bullshit Baffles Brains,' and I quickly saw why this was his mantra. The dictionary created irony from this I am sure. He would continually splurge outrageous claims of investment returns that were hyped, generic and lacked any detail or proof. Everything would be 'the next big thing,' a 'HUUUUUUGE opportunity you MUST get in NOW, Ohhhhh YES,' or, best and most frequently of all:

'We're all going to be MIIIIIIIIILLIONAIRES! Ohhhhh YES!''

Of course all of which lacked any credibility or proof. I could smell Horse shit emanating from every pore. Weirdly, I found it all harmless and amusing at first, cartoon like and naive, and his broad northern accent gave it a comedy factor that, in the early days, gave him a harmless, almost-but-not-quite affable quality. However, this wouldn't last long.

I once took him for dinner with Sam, who had recently bought a property at auction and made money flipping it. Chris spent the dinner pointing at Sam saying at 'auction equals caution.' Sam still reminds me of this today with a sarcastic smile slapped across his face. The reality was that Sam had done very well from his auction purchases understanding from experience what Chris had got confused in a book that he hadn't finished. Chris bamboozled Burty (Sam) through the dinner with his system of the more you say something and force it on people, the more they will believe you. Sam's nose instantly detected the shit odour.

Chris's selling strategy was based on 'hyper-excitement.' He would dismiss any facts or diligent questions as 'negativity,' barging and bullying through a pitch as if people would just be spun dizzily around into getting their credit cards out. Despite his ability to 'whip people into a frenzy,' I could see he lacked fundamental knowledge, even in my early investing years. The more of this excitement he built, the more it alarmed my Bullshit-ometer, but many people seemed to buy it. It was at a time where the market was growing, confidence was high, and I think the media and people's desire to get into property all gave him a backwind. People will believe what they want to believe, and Chris seemed to find people who wanted to believe him. I have to give him credit for that.

Despite my doubts from the outset, I wanted more than anything in the world to create a significant property portfolio and make money investing. It looked to me as though Chris was making a success of this to some level, I had seen some proof of deals such as the Hampton one I sold for a profit, and I couldn't help but think to myself, 'if he can do it, I definitely can too.' So I researched some of the property stock he had, worked the values out, and bought a property in Fosse Road in Leicester, off plan, for a £3,000 finders fee from Chris. He also wanted a 5% deposit to be paid to his 'sourcer' Adrian (who I later found out was the developer of that unit too). I decided that the 5% deposit should be paid to the solicitor on exchange, and not directly into Adrian's bank account(!). Chris quickly backed down and allowed me to keep the '5% deposit.'

*[NOW]. This property still hasn't been converted, 9 years later. Adrian had allegedly done a deal with a local Indian Restaurateur to buy St. Augustine's Church, however he had not exchanged contracts, had no planning permission, in fact had no more claim to the land/property than a random pedestrian walking by and claiming it because they saw it first. The promises that the development would be ready continued for some years, which came*

*to nothing. If I'd have paid the '5% deposit,' this would have gone up in smoke, as did most of Adrian's deal monies. Chris resisted paying my 'finders fee,' back for years, delusional that the development would 'be ready soon.' Once finally admitting it would never be built and the refund was due, 'next month,' was his standard line. In the end, once I'd started working for him, he linked it to how many sales I'd do in a month, as some kind of reward incentive. 'Sell 3 deals this month and you can have your money back.' This made me very angry, and with inflation, cost of capital and the time and energy it took to get that money back, it was probably worth about 35 pence to me once I finally got it.*

*The whole industry was teaming with these sort of 'riding the crest of a wave,' type people. It taught me to dig into the background of people and do my research thoroughly on what I was buying beforehand. I learnt not to buy off plan and only put deposits into solid properties which I could investigate at the time. It was fast paced and you could easily get confused or frenzied into buying all sorts of dreams that would have a shaggy dog story reality. I've not seen such hype and excitement in a market, and although the energy and optimism are good, you can easily let emotions sidetrack your logic and decision making.*

## No Career Envy

The turning point at ABP and the cross-roads I was staring at; one foot in work and the other foot in property and business, was looking at the higher level managers at 50 years old, driving VW Passats, earning no more than £50K a year with 40% tax deducted, and I knew I didn't want any of that.

I couldn't get particularly inspired by the life that they had carved out for themselves. I wanted mentors I could follow, but couldn't get excited by a £300k house and trips to the Dominican Republic. I just knew my fate laid ahead of me if I continued on the same path as all these mangers, and I still needed to give a lot of sweat to get there. It just didn't seem worth it to me. I had no problem, in fact I loved the idea of hard work and giving my time and commitment to something, but it had to be worthwhile. It had to be big. I had lost motivation and the time had come to break the structure my Dad had always wanted for me (and had for himself his entire life), and go out on my own in the world of business.

By this point I had two groups of friends: one group from my days at Kings School Peterborough, a non fee paying ex Grammar school, and another group from my days at Oakham, a full scale private boarding school. The difference in their parents' philosophies and direction through life was huge. My Kings' friends parents were accountants, Doctors, senior management; but in contrast my friends' fathers' from Oakham mostly had little or no education, but many with personal wealth that I estimated in excess of £10-20Million a piece. In fact, some in the hundreds of millions; almost all created from their own trading businesses, and most some mix of property and business in their wealth strategy. It became crystal that there was only one way to get the lifestyle I desired, and it wasn't through working for anyone else. And it wasn't through the traditional route most people are led to believe or influenced by their parents.

I'd already sniffed around Chris and was getting more involved in his property business. I'd bought a handful of properties myself which I enjoyed far more than any job, and Chris had let me know that he was looking for another 'shareholder,' as he called it, in Acorn – the new company he set up on his own, separate to his previous partner in 'Property Dogs.'

(Side note: the name 'Property Dogs,' still makes me laugh to this day. I don't think Chris knew how apt the name was, and I can't see how any serious business person would name a company like that. I wonder if he had a partner business called 'Property Wolves,' under a group of companies called 'Property Vultures?').

The deal that Chris force fed me was that to become part of Acorn, I HAD to buy shares. Ohhhhh YES! As I wanted in so badly, and my ears were somewhat happy, I agreed to buy in, paying a figure of around £1,000 per percentage point of the shareholding of the company. This was calculated by Chris's napkin valuation model. And I don't mean metaphorically; he'd literally take a napkin or beer mat from the pub we were meeting in and pitch his ideas. 'There you go, and you can keep it!' I thanked his (each time) and then asked to see the accounts, which to be honest I didn't really understand at the time. This was the only occasion when Chris dragged it out and grudgingly gave them to me. In true 'Bullshit Baffles Brains' mantra, Chris was railroading me that the company was a 'MUUUUUUULLLLLti-million pound cuuuutting EDGE cuuuuuuumpany,' and there were several millions of 'back-end' fees to rain in from the sky. (but I couldn't have any of the old ones, only the new ones).

In truth, I just wanted in really badly, and didn't really care. I saw this as my 'entrance fee,' something we'll discuss a lot, and the main driver for buying into Acorn was to learn deeply about this world of property investment. In the end I gave him £15,000 for '15% of the company,' which was negotiated back from the £40,000 that he wanted from me based on his multi-million napkin valuation. After countless arguments, bullying and desperation tactics, £15,000 was agreed.

After more wrestling, I negotiated with Chris that he'd pay me a minimum salary. I managed to get around £30K a year, which netted at around £2K per month. Chris's behaviour was so unbelievably erratic and unpredictable, and my gut was screaming at me not to trust him, but I needed the break to get into the industry and really understand how the investments worked. I need to see it from the inside; the inner workings and details, because that's the only way to get to the reality. My way around this internally/mentally was that I would live on a grand, save a grand, and use the savings to 'pay back' the capital I'd invested in Acorn (in reality just given to Chris to spend on depreciating financial liabilities). Over time and with some good sales, Chris put my salary up and I got quite quickly up to £53K per year. In less that 9 months I'd found a way to pay myself back on my initial investment. I can't say I'd totally worked it off, as I had to cut living expenses and carry on living at home, but it helped any concerns I had over getting that money back and the financial risk of the situation.

*[NOW] This proved to be a good decision, both financially and for my emotions. I managed to 'de-risk' working with Chris. Getting a good salary with regular chunky commission payments (whilst I was still in his good books), and creating a savings/investment strategy to pay the capital invested back, ensured I got an eye-opening, on the ground education for what turned out to be only an investment of time. This 'free' education at this time was one of the most valuable experiences I have EVER had. This was a vital lesson in doing deals, and to this day we ensure that every deal or business plan is de-risked, such that if it ends early or doesn't work out, any capital (or time) invested is paid back or covered. You gain infinite ROI once your capital is paid back, and in this deal it was essential for me because Chris's inconsistent, turbulent and brutal nature, and his frequent promises of huge cash lumps and back end windfalls had to be given the credence they deserved: zilch. I had to protect the downside, and ensure my capital and*

*time were covered regardless of the empty future promises. They had to be recognised as 'bonuses,' only and not depended upon.*

*I fully endorse this strategy of getting your own, Entrepreneurial 'management scheme,' training. Find an Estate Agency, or a company like Progressive Property, and offer to work for free, or actually get an employed job for 6-24 months. This will be infinitely better than any tradition education, and will accelerate at warp-speed your on the ground learning and experience in the real world you are entering. Plus it is a lot cheaper than a degree; you can 'earn while you learn,' and get the detailed nuances; the 5% that most don't know that makes 500% difference in results. I got some eye-wateringly valuable lessons at Acorn, sometimes just through being a fly on the wall, that no lecturer on the planet would or could teach you.*

## Training vs. Education

My new role was as Chris's 'business partner,' after all I had purchased shares, though in truth I was a glorified employee. My job was to get on the phones and sell the properties for finders fees. You can imagine Chris's induction and training process when entering the company: "You're sitting there, here's some leads, now get on the phone and SEEEEEELLLLL!" Ohhhhh YES! There were no processes, manuals, instructions, brochures or figures on the deals I was supposed to be selling. Initially Chris had me selling his dream properties in Florida. It was £27,500 down (as a fee, not a deposit) for a 3 bed villa supposedly valued at $375,000. Simple.

*(NOW) Looking back at it now, it is so clear to me that Chris was selling 'dreams' more than investments; the high cost low life. The main issues were that the rents never covered the mortgages and associated costs (homeowners association, property taxes, maintenance) and Chris's*

*projections of occupancy rates were optimistic at best. I think the reason that it took me longer than it usually would to get to the bottom reality of many of the deals being sold was that Chris would buy them all himself (as I did some myself). I really think that he has told so many people so many times that they were going to make millions that Chris believed his own BS. I was also blinded by my own hunger to learn on the job, in the early months. I put this down to my 'on the ground,' education, that I am grateful for.*

*To be fair to Chris, this was pretty normal in an industry where it was taken for granted that properties would keep going up and up and up for ever and ever. There were so many new build, off plan and overseas sourcing companies punting their wares, that I guess Chris thought his main advantage was to make them sound bigger and better than all the others. Trouble is, that is what everyone was doing. The dream sale got bigger and bigger, and virtually every sunny country or island in the world became the next and newest big-thing-hot-spot, or as Chris called it, 'the next eeeeeexxxxxPLOSIVE market.' Through the late 90's all the way through to the mid 2000's, the market just kept flying. Literally anyone could make money in property, it didn't matter about the upfront fees or the (lack of) income (yields), because the 20% growth in the next twelve months would cover it all and leave a nice big cash lump to pull out on top. Chris must have believed this himself, otherwise why would he put his name down for them all, and to that end I guess I have to respect his belief in what he was selling. Like most at this time, he probably thought the market growth would just keep going up, and it was easy to justify bad long term decisions to yourself. Though when he went to sleep at night, I'm not sure it all sat that well, because in the end it didn't with me (and that was the beginning of the end in this world). I was starting to learn the real, sustainable investing methods, and I'm looking forward to sharing them with you throughout the rest of this book.*

*Despite all the stories I am about to tell you about Chris and Acorn, working* for someone like him in a company like his gave me a real insider's view of the industry I never would have gotten through any institution or management training scheme. In fact a bigger, more credible business may not have given me the initial chance, or allowed me to do so much and be so involved ant the root source level so quickly. I got to learn so fast what works and what doesn't in property and business. I would say that what I learned in 12-18 months there would have taken me a decade through any other channel. I saw the good, the bad and the ugly. I got to the source of the sourcers, met clients and customers and dealt with them personally. I met business people way ahead of me, investors and developers worth significantly more than me; all giving me valuable peeping Tom insights and on the job experience.

I learned my coalface education in the best (worst) time. Because the market was going crazy, barriers to entry were virtually non existent. Anyone could set up a property business with zero qualifications or regulation. Novices and speculators were making silly money, and people without big experience (like me) could get in deep and early. Had I got in heavy in 2003, I may have had my 'foundational training' in a time that would have taught me all the wrong long term fundamentals, and it may have been the case that by the time the market crashed I could have been too big or too deep to recover. Thankfully my timing of entry into the market was actually fortuitously good, though at the time it seemed like the worse time. I got in not too long before the big crash, and virtually all the established companies dropped like flies. More on that later, but for now just remember that you must make the deal work from the start, and not buy on the hope of future growth. The deal should work if you hold it for 25 years. Capital growth will come (extremely likely according to history), but when and how much **_can't be predicted by anybody_**.

## "Totally ExxxxxxCLUUUSIVE" Florida Deals

These Florida deals Chris would have me selling were "totally

ExxxxxxCLUUUSIVE." This became his main selling line. They had sooooo many amazing investment benefits such as splash pools, mosquito netting, clubhouses and ten minutes from the gates of Disney: stuff that he was convinced to his core being were of huge benefit, but I saw as totally irrelevant in making serious investment decisions. Whenever I'd mention 'yield,' for example, Chris would chastise me continually: 'You won't get a YIELD on these deals!' he would say. I think what he meant to say is that you wont get cashflow. Him not understanding one of the most fundamental terms in property investment as yield further reduced my respect for him. 'People want capital growth and these are going to EXPLODE!'

Chris had never even been to Florida, and I think I got one of my most eye opening, fly-on-the-wall documentary style lessons when I went out to Florida and Nevis with Chris to meet the developers to understand the developments. Chris wanted me to pay for my own expenses, despite wanting me to go, so I managed to get a good cheap time share deal from my then Girlfriend's Mum; a small one bed apartment, for a week for £150 in the middle of the park zone in Orlando. I saw this as an investment in my knowledge, but didn't see the need to waste money on accommodation I'd hardly be staying in. Chris made me sleep on the sofa bed in the Living room while he took the double bed, and every night he'd enforce upon me that we were to go out and hit the local bars and clubs.

When we arrived on site I was expecting to see a building, or at least some building works, but after months of 'promising to break ground,' they still hadn't started. Chris's version of '10 minutes to Disney gates,' must have been via Concord, and Chris barely wanted to look around the development or get to know the developer. He was more interested in going and looking around 'Champions Gate,' and 'Reunion,' other developments in the area, to force me to invest in one 'with him.' I really felt that he was trying to get more money out of me to lock me into his web and exercise more control of me. The more money I would give him, the harder I would find it to leave, and the more Chris could get me to respond to his militant orders.

I figured out while in Florida that the average purchasing/transaction costs were about 10% of the price of the property. If you're selling a property, the two realtors will take a 6% commission. That is so much more than the UK, and the structure of the purchase and sale are worlds apart. The realtors (US Estate Agent) do the legal work, whereas in the UK this is done by specialist solicitors. It seemed to me that the system in the US nurtured a huge conflict of interest in that your realtor, who had a vested interest in pushing the sale through, would be the one advising you on the legal contract with the developer you were buying the property from. Where is the incentive for the realtor to advise you of any contract conflicts or irregularities (or illegalities), when they are getting 6% or more (sometimes 10% to 15% from new build developers) from the sale?! This different legal system was one way that UK resellers could baffle you into dream-like overseas developments.

This structure would be fine in an environment where the sellers and purchasers understood the rules. Indigenous people would understand this system that seemed so strange to me, but I saw herds of English people buying in Florida through a system they didn't understand; they were like Lambs to the slaughter. Contracts which they were advised to sign by the realtors (frequently taking $50,000 plus in commissions from the sale of new build properties), were littered with ways for the purchasers to lose out, including unlimited delivery timescales and prices which weren't fixed. If the market went up the developer could whack up your purchase price, after you'd paid your deposit, and in so many unheard of ways in the UK you could lose your purchase/deposit.

*[NOW] Local markets vary wildly with their rules and systems. If there is 4,000 miles, mostly consisting of sea, between your market and the market you are looking to buy in, then there will be that relative amount of difference in the purchasing, selling and legal systems. These trips to the US and Nevis really drilled into me that you are at a huge disadvantage investing in far away markets you don't understand. You have to pay your 'entrance fee,' all over again, and for the entire time (until you become an expert) you are totally exposed. Why not get brilliant in one (or two) (local) markets. And we haven't even touched on management and maintenance yet; just the purchasing process.*

*These differences only benefit the developers, who can use this lack of knowledge from the 'investors,' to push up (or make up) prices, and baffle their 'diligence.' I have seen this countless times. You have less control the further away you are, and you are helplessly in reliance of the local developer and reseller, who all have huge ulterior motives. You see this in reverse a lot in London. There's so much foreign money flying in, with overseas investors overpaying because they don't know the local market and price comparables (comps). The pay the prices pitched to them (more than local investors pay) and are again totally reliant on the local resellers and managers to advise them well and manage the properties properly.*

*Inevitably the market in Florida began to unwind in '06-'07. Some of the areas that we had been looking at dropped in value by around 80% from top to bottom (!). Even in crash/recession in the UK, the biggest drops were around 30% for existing property. In 2009 it was like a big fire sale as the banks weren't lending. I saw so many apocalyptic casualties. I had personally put deposits down on multiple villas before I got these valuable lessons, some of which I managed to get back and some of which I lost. Another 'entrance fee.' Chris would try and pressure me into buying more through him, so that he could go and spend the money on Hugo Boss suits that were too tight and Bang & Olufsen stereo equipment he never used. It seemed to make him feel good in the moment.*

## Nevis & Butthead

Chris was also selling properties on the Caribbean Island of Nevis, and by the time we got there he'd pretty much persuaded me to take one of the Villas. He told me that the developer was selling them for $1.2M, and that he had bank valuations of $1.7M. Something didn't feel right, but having met the developer previously in Florida, and seeing a test valuation on one of the Villa's, I became a lot more interested. When we walked out of a meeting with the developer I said to Chris 'I think I'll have one of those Villa's,' for which I would have to pay Chris £50,000 in fees for (yes I know it sounds crazy now but that's what he used to try and do!). Chris's reaction at this point made me shudder with repulsion and I'll never ever forget it: I could see Chris visibly salivating. He shook and shuddered, rubbed his hands together violently with evil excitement, and his body reacted as though he'd just had a shot of pure adrenaline. He went all red and sweaty and couldn't hide his celebration. It was like I was his prey. He had got me. This made me even more concerned.

At the end of the trip I decided to tell Chris that I was going to Nevis to look at the Villa's, while we were on the deck chairs by the pool. He totally freaked out, 'Whhhhhyy do you need to view them? What difference will it make?!' He pointed at me aggressively and went very red in the face. He told me I had riiiiiidiculous ideas. 'WHAT are you wasting money on those flights for?' It was clear to me by his reaction that he knew that when I got there, I would change my mind. I also think he probably felt guilty that he wouldn't do this kind of research, and wouldn't want me coming back with more knowledge – he'd lose his grasp of control over me that he thought he had. This made me want to go even more.

*[NOW] I kept ignoring the terrible, awful feeling I had about this deal because of the glitter of all the equity. I have since learned, and often the hard way (i.e. making mistakes myself and losing money; my 'entrance fees') that if I don't feel good about any business or investment, I simply wouldn't get into it. I know it is easy to say it with hindsight and without the emotion of the decision at hand, but there are so many opportunities that will come your way that you don't need to take ridiculous risks. You should trust your feeling and not get allured by that that shines. I've had so many sleepless nights worrying about investments I've made or was looking at making, that didn't feel right. If it's too good to be true, it's too good to be true.*

So I decided to travel to Nevis, costing me £600, to do diligence on the Villa I was considering buying from Chris. One of the only ways I could stop Chris going completely mad was because there were some left to sell, and so I could lead him to believe I would sell them for him. The trip was a bit of an adventure, as I had to go via Puerto Rico, and when I arrived on the Island I realised how remote and undeveloped it was. Granted, it was a hideaway for the rich and famous, but there were less than 5 restaurants on the *entire* Island, and it made me think that it was very inaccessible and couldn't have much tourist traffic. It didn't take me long, thinking back to my supply demand curve modules at University to think 'how are we going to rent these out?' The enormity of the purchase price, and therefore debt to service, further concerned me. Surely I should be starting small and working my way up.

*[NOW] Both the Florida and Nevis trip gave me undeniable evidence that you never know what any market looks like until you go there. How I pictured these developments, how they were portrayed in the glossy brochures and*

how Chris would sell them were of dreams for films, and a far cry from the stone cold reality. Diligence should always involve getting hands on with your research: go and view the properties (or have a trusted advisor), meet the people involved, talk to everyone, see it and touch it. It was only when I stepped off the plane and set foot on the footings that I got a real sense of timescales of builds, knowledge of local developers, regulations, ideas of rental values, voids, maintenance and other essential information to make a smart investment decision.

The huge purchase price of the Nevis Villa scared me silly. When you pass your driving test, most normal people don't drive a Bugatti out of the test office. If you are going to bump and scrape a car, put the wrong fuel in it, get it insured or cause a minor accident, it is better in a £46 Nova than a £1,000,000 hypercar. The same is true for investing. I see people all the time with eyes bigger than their belly, and they scale up too quick, or jump in too deep. Cut your teeth and start small. You get to make all the (necessary) mistakes in a relatively safe and comfortable environment, with the lowest possible 'entrance fees,' and learn your trade without having your pants pulled down. You get the opportunity to learn and get better, and you get to make mistakes and tests on smaller units/investments that give you valuable lessons that don't involve learning about bankruptcy.

Becoming a master investor is about constant refinement and evolution. Small tweaks and tests performed multiple times over a longer period of time create giant and compounded improvements in the long term. Fast and instant giant leaps whilst appealing, often end in poor quality investments. Leverage the knowledge of others, like you are reading this, to reduce your 'entrance fee,' even more. The better a mentor is and the bigger 'entrance fees,' they've had, the lower yours will be, as you get the mistakes and fees vicariously, and not for real for yourself.

I found a realtor in Nevis who was completely unconnected with the developer who Chris was dealing with (in Nevis). I got him to show me round some other developments and go through the expected rental returns and sale prices. My unbiased research proved that none of the comps stacked up against any of the Villa's Chris was trying to sell me, and the rental occupancy levels (as usual) fell way below required levels to anywhere near cover running costs. The realtor candidly explained to me that these were primarily holiday homes and not investments. I spent 2 sleepless nights trying to work out how I was going to tell Chris that I wouldn't be investing. I played his cartoon like response over and over in my mind.

When I returned, I bottled a little and fabricated a story that I needed some of the fees from William (my stepfather), and he was no longer willing to invest. Chris took this opportunity to proclaim that he never liked William anyway. He got his usual red faced and steamy eared, and blurted that 'William is aaaaaaallways throwing a spanner in the works.' I could see that he'd already spent my £50,000 finders fee on the new Bang & Olufsen rotating TV he didn't know how to use and the latest Paul Smith suit that was designed for people 20 years younger than him.

*[NOW] Going around Nevis with the developer taught me a most valuable lesson I carry around with me at all times: ulterior motives. As the realtor was unconnected to this development, he had no vested interest to warp the sense of truth and judgment. Everyone has their own agenda and ulterior motive, which I have no issue with, but to get sound knowledge to base your personal investment decisions on, you either need to be fully aware of what the ulterior motives are (so you can add your measured dose of salt), or get to a source where none exist, where most of the truth is hidden.*

*People, myself included in my Nevis experience, get totally blinded by the glitz, razzamatazz and dream of the overseas market; mixing 'investment,' with the emotional excitement of a 'holiday home.' We make illogical and instant fix decisions when emotional, and this totally hides the reality that the market is never the same as the one you are in, and what you don't know will hurt you. It is so much easier and more cost effective to continue to improve in the markets that you know and are local to, even if they are not the next 'up and coming,' boomtown, because you can control the most fundamental issues. Booms are cyclical by area and come and go. Predicting them is futile, and in attempting to, the rules and fundamentals of investing are being overlooked.*

*Conversely, my Dad was skeptical to an obsessive degree. I have learned to temper the extreme skepticism, because you never end up actually making any investments or setting up your businesses. But a fair and reasonable dose of skepticism, until proven otherwise, is smart when making decisions involving your or investors' time and money. In life, be positive and optimistic by all means, have big dreams and goals, but in investment start skeptical, don't be too 'happy ears,' for all the good signs, and dig as deep as you can to the unbiased reality. Then, once you have given yourself the green light, you have a much greater chance of making some money, and you can be aggressively 'positive.'*

## MLM & HYIP's

Chris was in his mid to late 40's, and I was in my mid 20's when I was at Acorn. Our 'partnership,' was more a dictatorship, where I did all the work under strict military orders, while he drank countless espresso's which completely dictated his mood. He'd spend hours a day scouring the 'net for the latest scheme or network marketing opportunities. I specifically remember 'Reality Millions,' which became 'Divinus Opulentia,' (a HIYP – High Income Yielding Program – or Ponzi in my book). These get rich quick schemes promised huge levels of interest, often into the double digits per month, all with their own 'rationale,' or story to create these eye-watering returns. These ranged from clicking ads to 'generate ad revenue,' a new crack team of offshore forex traders who'd found a 'loophole in the system,' and precious metals about to 'go ballistic.' Chris was totally addicted to these. He spent most of his day 'researching' these opportunities (happy clicking and daydreaming), instead of actually working in his (our) business, and he'd regularly bound out of his office on a fresh caffeine high and announce to the whole office "I've found it. This is the very latest, newest and cuuuuuuutting edge money making system that will make us instant mmmmmiiiiiillionaires!" He would order me to down tools selling properties for him, and sell his new scheme to investors. Of course when all of these schemes were new, he would be near the top of the 'tree,' in true pyramid fashion. I would humour him for a few days ignoring them until he'd be onto the next one.

He 'invested,' well into 5 figure sums, thoroughly believing he would get 4 times his money back in a few months time. I would frequently put the expected pay out dates that Chris had publicly declared, into my mobile phone calendar, and when the reminder pinged up I would watch his demeanour that day. He'd often be pissed off and take it out on me. I'd strategically wait a week to question him on it, and his favourite line was 'they've had a problem with their payment processor' (often e-Gold, another concept I find amusing). Chris dragged countless people into these programs, earning commission from their capital being at the top of the tree, and over time I watched every single one of these people, including Chris, lose all of their money. In hindsight, I believed that all of these Ponzi schemes sometimes paid out for a period to lure more and bigger money in, but the investment returns would always end one way: total capital destruction. High cost, low life. An unaffordable life of (ultimate) poverty.

# The Whipping Boy

Because Chris was of a military and police upbringing, his management style was of orders and commands: and you were to always obey rank. Of course this made me want to break away from him and set up on my own, and Dad's rebellious genes kicked in, but there were huge hidden benefits to this. The main one was that because he was getting me to do all the work while he sat in his Ivory Tower, I learned just about everything in the entire chain of property investing. I never would have gotten close in a more corporate environment with more employees and a more rigid and deep org chart. I've learned that if I (you) have a clear goal, dream or objective in mind, you can accept short term discomfort for your long term result. I despised being Chris' whipping boy, but not as much as not achieving business and investing success, so it was a small and short term price to pay.

I learned which developers to go to and which ones were malleable for a deal – the larger scale builders that did entry-level units. No small developer would give volume discounts in the same way, and often their buildings were too highly priced and didn't work on a yield calculation. I learned at what level to make contact with them. Often the lady in the sales office would be the entry in and she would need schmoozing, but ultimately you are after the contact of the sales manager/director for the region. At this level you would also be offered stock around the whole region, often focusing on their sites where sales were low. You could get better discounts by helping them clear sites that hadn't sold. If you could completely clear a development and take all the remaining units, ending that developers commitment to the site and closing the show home, you could get the best level of discounts.

Knowing which times of the year to approach them was a key advantage in your knowledge armoury. The types of developers I dealt with were national players and were therefore listed on the stock exchange. Because of this they had rigid reporting mechanisms and time periods, which were welded to the senior managements' bonuses and remuneration. If the sales director felt like he could include a large lump of sales (ten units plus) before the end of a reporting period (quarter, half year or year end), you could pull his pants down on price. Each developer had different reporting timeframes, and I'd log these once I dug them out, and diarise them on my mobile calendar with a reminder 8 weeks before. I'd pounce at this time and get the best prices. This was supposed to be Chris's job, but I was loving sucking up all this knowledge and so cracked on both in work hours and in my spare time.

Although not a viable investing strategy in todays market, going straight to the developer and securing bulk discounts could again come into play in a growing market. Whilst gaining all this knowledge I was also testing other models of property investment, especially existing/2nd hand properties in different local, micro areas. Again, I was able to do this because of the free reign I was 'given,' at Acorn, having all the other models that Chris was implementing to test against. Would I have gotten this seven management levels down in a big company? Unlikely.

## Marketing & Lead Generation

Although my job was officially Chris's partner, he made it my responsibility to 'generate leads.' When I started, I didn't even know what that meant, but was thrown in the deep end (again, a secondary benefit) and learned quickly on the job. Chris dragged me to various networking events and I saw an underground, cult-like frenzy of people drooling over the next get rich quick super-fad. One of Chris's friends he had imposed himself upon, Michael, was involved with a secret 'underground tipster.' It was a membership subscription of tipping Horses to win races. You'd get regular new tips from this tipster based in Spain, in return for a subscription. He would then get on stage at the events and start selling the service to 'suspects,' and Chris, in true fashion, started dragging people in and placing bets on the horses through the service.

We later found out that a group of them travelled to Spain to see the 'tipster.' One of the women involved had worked out the source of the tips, as there was an amazingly close correlation between the secret tipster's recommendations and the tips in the Sun racing section. No joke. A female member of the group managed to grab hold of the tipster and kick him in the shins with her pointy shoes. He later vanished, probably to Cyprus. I couldn't believe my eyes that people were selling 'betting,' schemes as investments, but it gave me confidence to sell property deals because they were far more likely to get a return, even if the deals weren't great, or were abroad, as long as it was seen as a long term investment.

Chris couldn't get his head around the fact that get rich quick schemes don't exist. I started to see with my own eyes that Chris was as addicted to the dream as he was the reality of making any real and sustainable money. He needed the instant hit of the next big thing to help him feel good about himself, and hide the cracks of what was really going on in his life financially and emotionally.

Despite this craziness, there were actually a good amount of quality leads and good people who attended networking events, and it was a relatively cheap way of drumming up business. It was also a good way to see what others were selling, meeting contacts, sourcers and business people with interesting investing models. It really keeps you on the front line of what's happening in the markets, what people are selling and what investors are hungry for. To this day I see networking and events as a staple diet, not just in generating leads but as a gateway to great contacts and to stay at the early mover stage of market movements. I have many great, wealthy, smart and connected people in my network now from the early meetings I attended, or at least through them, all at the relatively low cost of attending these events (many paid on expenses by Chris/Acorn, so I have to be grateful for that).

I was also involved in the more innovative marketing strategies, as a small company always should be. Back then we didn't have social media which has made lead generation easier than ever, but the birth of PPC (Pay Per Click) was about to change the face of marketing. Of course Chris was excited because it was new, but had no idea how to use the system properly. Chris would pay someone to 'generate leads,' and £500 later I'd have nine sheets of paper laid out across my desk with Chris jumping up and down shouting 'SELL SELL SELL.' These people would have tentatively shown an interest in buying overseas and I had to 'cllllllllllllOSE them ALL,' like someone would put an email address in a page and then pay £50,000 to someone they didn't know for an overseas investment in Nevis!

Although I was an untrained salesperson, I quickly learned that if you kept following up on people, speaking to them regularly, building a personal and trusting relationship, you could get some success, and you didn't need techniques or gimmicks. I was not like Chris, selling on pure excitement, I liked to build the trust, giving the client specific information and facts of the level and quality of the developments, and give them details on the factors that made the deals a good investment. As the market was rising through the early to mid 2000's, people were hungry for property, both in the UK and overseas, and so this was a relatively smooth process. In the 18 months I was at Acorn I sold over

100 property deals, mainly in the UK but some abroad. It was an eye opening experience both positively, and also in how to sell only what you believe in, which I will come to later.

## Summary

I've learned the fastest route of least resistance is down a path someone else has trodden. The route that someone else has trodden, gone through all the hurdles, fallen down all the mines, taken all the wrong routes, got lost, stuck, started going backwards, sideways and all ways. And they've gone back through that entire journey, plotting the shortest route that misses all these diversions. Someone's done that in your chosen niche or industry. Someone's spent decades doing it, with all the battle scars they can show off to you to prove it. Be careful of get rich quick – sit-on-a-Beach-drinking-Pina-Colada-in-Marbella-and-come-back-a-millionaire instant results. They don't exist and be very careful of taking someone else's words when it comes to parting with your hard earned cash.

# 9. Caffeine addictions & acorns to oaks

Chris was a big drinker. He was a creature of habit and would have many pints of Lager every night, always pulling me out of the office a little early to go to the Wetherspoon's pub conveniently located opposite our office: the Draper's Arms. He would enforce me to go out with him most weekends because he didn't have anyone to go out with, and he'd stand in Nightclubs ogle-ing over girls less than half his age, telling me graphically what he was going to do to them back in the office once the clubs had shut.

On many a Monday morning I would arrive early to the office to find empty Champagne bottles and ladies clothes strewn across the office meeting table and window sill. Chris would have a smug look on his face as he arrived to the office about 45 minutes after me as if to say 'look what I got up to over the weekend.' Penny, our office managers' face would tell a more pertinent story.

Every lunchtime without fail Chris would go and order the same sandwich, muffin and coffee from Starbucks. His habits die hard, and he found it hard to find new things and venture out. I would stand in that bloody queue every day while Chris ordered a Chicken and Bacon sandwich, Skinny Blueberry Muffin (as if it made any difference!) and large Americano, thinking that there must be more to life than this Groundhog day reality. Even today I don't like going into Starbucks because it reminds me of how he made me feel. Chris started doing his own events to sell his new opportunities, and it would be my responsibility to 'fill the room.' He would 'sell from the stage,' and I used to sit at the back of the room, operating the projector and serving the bottled water and cringe. It was like a 1985 infomercial without the sales skills. A hybrid of the cheapest shopping channel you've ever seen and a Steve Coogan or David Brent office character. But this did get me to understand the importance of running events, which I'll come to later. I'd carry the laptop and Dell computer speakers from Holiday Inn to Holiday Inn, with cheap and chintzy pop up stands with dollar bills flying all over them and Chris standing there with his arms open and an hypnotic gaze into your eyes. Chris's sales method was to bully everyone into signing up:

'This it TOOOOOOOTALLY above board this one is, the Queen's Council have been right the way through it so let me declare, this is NOT a scam. I repeat, this is NOT a scam!' I am sure you don't need me to add any statements that point out the irony in this.

'Everyone who thinks this is a scam can leave now. Right, everyone who's left, 'we've established Ladies and Gentlemen that this is NOT a scam.'

He would use market trader type sales techniques to try and induce people to buy. 'You won't find this cheaper AAAAAANYWHERE else! The growth in Florida is going to be EXPLOOOOOOSIVE! Nevis is TOOOOOTALLY exclusive. All the footballers are buying in Nevis so you MUUUUUST buy one NOW!' To Chris, the most important sales technique was based on people having bragging rights with their friends on who has the biggest Condo. Or maybe there's another word for it.

While we were running these events, Chris's new multi-level marketing scheme, called LogicL, was based on selling wealth creation information for a sign up and monthly fee. Whilst the wealth creation books and videos contained within the online platform were quite good, they could be accessed from somewhere like Amazon or a book shop independently. While Chris was selling this I simply couldn't understand how he, or anyone, would ever make enough money to make it worth their time. It would take as much effort for Chris to drag people into the office to sell them this for £50 a month, as it was to sell a Villa in Florida for £25,000. At least people believe in property and have seen the undeniable proof for decades. At least many wealthy people have made serious long term wealth from property. But pyramids and ponzis and some (not all) network marketing were both a difficult thing to sell and had such negative perception around them, often for good reason. And LogicL in particular, was based on 'membership' to gain information that I thought was freely available anyway. He did this time and time again. I think he thought he'd make 'passive income,' through the commissions, and extend his 'down line.' I always thought that if I was sitting in the audience, I would want to see actual real examples of people who've become super rich in MLM schemes. If it could be proven without doubt and by enough people, then fair enough. But they seemed thin on the ground to none existent. There were no examples of mentors who were helping people learn and become wealthy, and with all the effort it took, why not just do something that works and is proven?

*(NOW) This really showed me the importance of selling something that you believe in, that works, and most importantly, being able to show other people the proof. When we run Progressive events now, we make sure that we bring along the community members who are implementing the strategies we teach them. People need certainty and there are numerous schemes and scams that will part one and their money. Others who have succeeded through the training or mentorship of a service help alleviate risk and uncertainty in taking the next step and investing money and time. If you have something to hide, there won't be any of these, so it gives you a strategic selling advantage when you do. Sometimes at a Progressive event where we have 200 delegates, there could be an additional 50 or so community members who've bought properties and are making income. There are 100's*

*at our big events. You should be open and let your potential customers talk to them, in private. You should involve them in your sales process and not try to hide slight faults you have as it makes you more real and believable. People don't want perfection, they want real people willing to help.*

*Your best sales team is your customers, without a doubt. Get them selling for you, and you won't have to work as hard yourself. Plus your customers will always be believed more than you.*

All the people I met through Chris's schemes who were at the level above, selling the platforms from bigger stages with even more brash attitude, all seemed to be selling something they weren't doing. It made me very skeptical of anything that looked too good to be true. I would have much preferred to sell the property deals at these events, which I thought they were intended for, but Chris used to take over them, selling the delegates something they hadn't even come to see.

## That meeting

I met a guy at the bar after one of these events who'd been doing some work for Chris's friend Mike, who ran the local designer furniture shop. We'd discussed at the bar some properties we'd both looked at in a local area of Peterborough, and how they looked like good deals, and some of the books Chris was ramming down everyone's throats as a way for people to get out of their sorry existence and change their lives. I actually liked some of them, and gave him the recommendations. We exchanged cards, his name was Rob. This was Rob's first exposure to Chris and Acorn.

The next week Rob came into the office and said he'd read all of them. At first I didn't believe it, being somewhat skeptical in nature, and because most people talk more than do. But then I realised it was true as he recited their detailed points, quoting certain phrases and passages, and I couldn't believe someone had put all that work in; in fact I'd never seen it before; I think it was 3 books in that week. Rob was insistent that he wanted to stay close, in fact he 'popped' into the office most days, and as it transpired he got a job with us at Acorn with a recommendation from me and something that Chris saw in him too. He later told me he'd have worked for free, and I admired that desire. I could relate to this as I had wanted the knowledge more than the salary. I'd built a bit of a relationship with Rob outside Acorn and was getting on well with him, so I suggested to Chris that we give him a job, commission only, selling deals. Chris had also been really impressed, so he gave him a job with no salary at first. No risk to Acorn.

Rob was an artist at the time, and had some pictures exhibited in the furniture shop that Mike, Chris's friend ran. We also had our office above the shop, so there was a co-incidental link between us all. I would usually have dismissed someone's aptitude with zero experience, but Rob's desire made up for that. He became very good at selling the deals very quickly because of the time, effort and commitment that he put in. He was always reading or listening to CD's on the way to work, in the lunch break and in the evenings, and would always stay late at work. I could see him inserting phrases to clients straight out of the books, and he built confidence very quickly. Chris was blown away so gave him a more permanent position after a few weeks, with a wage and increased commissions.

*[NOW] Rob's application impressed upon me the value of immersing yourself and working harder than anyone else to get to a higher standard. He didn't have any knowledge when he started, but he read, studied, worked and stayed late to get up to speed very fast. If now I ever feel like*

*I know less than others, or I want to break into a new area, I know that if I immerse myself, read lots, talk to many others already doing it, I can move into it quickly and successfully. This was the first proof to me that knowledge and experience aren't the only factors to success, and it gave me a lot of confidence. A lot of people will worry about a lack of knowledge and it will affect their confidence, and Rob's example should give you the proof you need that you start with what you've got and use your enthusiasm, desire and passion as your main asset.*

*We have trained tens of thousands of investors through Progressive, and this is the asset that everyone has when they start, regardless of their knowledge or experience. Yet most student or 'newbies,' seriously underestimate the value of this hidden asset, and so it can take them longer to get up to speed. This single thing that will 'cover up,' or make up for a lack of knowledge and experience is this radiant desire, and you don't need to go on any course to learn that or have a high cost base.*

## Acorns to Oaks

Rob and I started selling together and sat next to each other at the other end of the office to Chris' glass tower. As time went on our relationship grew and I found it much easier to have support from an equal to balance Chris's emotional roller-coaster character. At a similar time, I'd started to see the reality of not only all of Chris's get rich quick deals (which were easy for me to avoid by focusing on the property sales), but actually how little diligence and research he did on the property deals, especially the overseas ones. In the crazy rising market these cracks would be smoothed over, but as things started to go wrong, my education took another stage, and I saw the beginning of the end for Acorn and my relationship with Chris. I'd always really believed in the property deals I was selling, as I would do my own research and diligence off my own back, behind Chris' back, as I wanted to sound credible to the clients and give them something tangible. Chris never wanted me doing research because I think it threatened him, but also he thought it took time away from selling. Of course I knew that it was easier to sell once you had good proof, and I'd focus on selling those deals only, brushing the ones Chris imposed upon me in other Universes, to one side. But once the market started to change, as it did in the mid 2000's, my life and lessons in education took a dramatic twist.

In the background from selling through Acorn, I was testing some deals myself that Chris refused to sell. He didn't want me having any life outside Acorn, and he certainly didn't want me independent enough to make my own decisions. These were older properties, dirtier, not new, and Chris hated them. But the valuations on the new builds would not match what they could be sold for, in *reality*, once they were no longer new, compared to the 'existing deals,' I'd been buying out of office hours (that I had to keep secret from Chris). The stark comparison made me want to focus solely on existing older units, much more able to give me a low cost high income, and not the new ones Acorn and everyone else in the UK had gone crazy over.

The new builds were more expensive than the local deals I was buying, with much higher service charges, especially the flats, even though they were new and shouldn't have needed such charges. Despite their newness, they could command virtually no more in rent, yet because they cost significantly more and needed higher mortgages, the yield, return and cashflow were a lot lower. It was so clear I felt I had found a sustainable model and was very excited.

I got Rob involved as a partner, and this drove us further apart from Chris, and closer together. We did approach him a few times with the 'new,' (old) model to bring into Acorn, as we knew we could sell it better and could see that things could go very wrong, but he'd dismiss it out of hand. 'Too much work. Uuuuuuugly. No one will want them.' Yet these offered all the things you want in an 'investment,' that the new builds, overseas and off plan's did not. I couldn't understand his disgust, yet he enforced that ANY deals we bought should be through the cuuuuuumpany, despite having no contract of any kind with him or Acorn. Because this was something we were scaling up, I had to keep schtuum; I certainly didn't want to own any properties with Chris. His attitude to credit was suicidally dangerous; buying unnecessary goods through the company on credit which I worried would end in tears later. He'd often exclaim: 'It's all about LEVERAGE. Leverage it RIGHT up to the max, it's like a cash machine!'

I recall a new build flat that Chris bought to live in. Of course, because it was new, it had all the bells and whistles; video telecom entry, plasma TV, brand new wooded flooring throughout, the latest appliances and more that the glossy brochures paraded. It was all very emotionally appealing, and from my Dad's upbringing, that was the signal to be cautious. This one flat the Chris reserved, with a value in excess of £350,000, has recently, 8 years later, been sold in a block at around £160,000 value; HALF it's initial (hyped) valuation nearly a decade later. Local houses that I bought in the same year have just passed 2007 values, having endured the biggest property crash, possibly ever. The older house is worth a little more, and the newer flat with the bells and whistles has just sold for less than half it's 2006 sale price! It is much harder to 'hype up,' the valuation of an older, 'existing,' house because the new, shiny, emotional triggers can't be used.

## More Addictions

One particular purchase alerted me to his lack of investment know how. Chris bought a £2,500 TV to hang on the wall in the new office (that no one ever visited) to play nothing more than a screensaver. With 5 minutes research he could have bought an equally good one with similar size and spec for £600. Even 8 years on £2,500 is at the very top end of TV prices. Chris thought that the way to buy a desktop computer for a new employee was to get a £2,000 top of the range Dell. The reality was that the £500 model would do exactly the same thing, but he didn't care because he put it all on credit and company expenses. I will show you proof later of how a few savings here can compound to a life long, job replacing income. I could never understand if Chris actually intended to ever pay for any of this stuff. Either way it concerned me to become financially connected to him through the UK credit system.

Other examples of this flippant attitude to credit was involved in his 'investments.' New build flats that Chris would source through Adrian, that after all costs would probably have negative cashflow of £500 to £1,000 per month! An industry term for this is 'under water,' well this is like a sunken

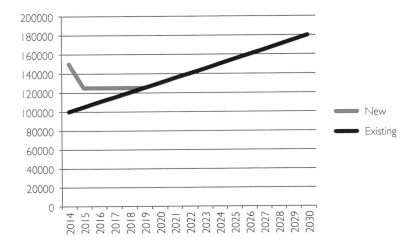

## Value of Car

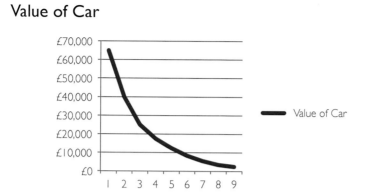

ship at the bottom of the Ocean. Chris would get very excited by the 'instant cashback,' on completion of up to £20,000. This was effectively the surplus of what the lender was lending, and what the developer was being paid for the property. Chris would see this as free money, and this short-termism ran through virtually all of his thinking. Getting effectively 100% mortgages and creating huge monthly cash shortfalls were not in my definition of investments, and I had the tested proof that you could make much more money at much lower risk and exposure on something down the road, not new.

## Summary

The full immersion experience in the early days— being with other property investors revolutionised everything I had 'already' learned from grey to vivid colour. The mistakes to avoid. The strategies to follow. I never deny myself the opportunity to learn something new from the internet, books or live events, just because I didn't do everything I learned yesterday. If I invest in education and the advice really pays off – then I know there's more where that came from. Take it all. Bathe in it. Whether consciously or unconsciously, you can only become it in the end.

# 10.Value in Local(ity)

Buying local, non new properties which I sourced from Estate Agents were giving me the same 'no money left in,' principle as had been first shown to me by Des. I could buy at a discount, add value through refurbishment, and remortgage up to a reasonable loan to value (LTV) percentage of the valuation price, effectively drawing back out any money I had put in without over exposing or leveraging (in the way that Chris loved). I could still make a margin when debt and costs had been taken off, as the mortgages on the properties were significantly lower but the rents were virtually the same on similar types. It's a lot like Chris's TV purchase – the £2,500 one did virtually nothing more than the £600 one other than drop in value like a boulder. I found that you could get a ten year old (or more) three bed house that served virtually the same purpose as an off plan or new build one, yet cost sometimes half as much.

This was quite a surprise to me, because you simply don't get older existing properties marketed to you as an investment as much as the new builds by the developers and property companies, especially in this booming market. I have since learned that the best opportunities often appear hidden to the masses. I guess this is because they are not as glitzy or glamorous. They also look to most like a lot more work in refurb and maintenance, which puts most people off. The fact that they are not new turns people off and gives them a false perception of hard graft, lower value, more costs and tenant issues. It is actually these exact concepts that make them more sound as an investment.

*(NOW) Most investors want to invest into something that they are emotionally connected to. They like the 'look and feel,' (bad investment principles/language) of it and would want to live there themselves and show*

their friends around it. You are not the tenant, however, and you would not necessarily want or have to live where they do. You are not your target market. Because renting out the properties fast and for long periods is as important as buying them well, you should always buy with the tenant in mind and where they would want to live, rather than you. Remember, you are not your tenant.

New build properties are like buying a new Car off the forecourt, they devalue as soon as you buy them. People pay more for new properties over existing properties probably because they are unblemished and can pick their favourite carpets, curtains, cooker, worktop and tiles, and people assume that there will be less maintenance issues. The reality is that in new properties you get new, lower quality boilers that go wrong very quickly, and often many of the heating systems, switches, locks and so forth are of a lower grade than an older property, and thus will require maintenance call outs. You also have snagging issues. When items are new and untarnished you pay a premium for them in tax, research and development (R&D), profit margins to the manufacturer, marketing costs and warranty, yet they are often no better than the same model or type a few years old but in the same generation and type. Over the years it has become harder for developers to make margins. The old days of 1/3 land cost, 1/3 build cost and 1/3 profit are long gone. Land is at a serious premium, and costs of materials and labour has risen. Because of this, the quality and size of build has reduced. You'll notice much smaller rooms that can hardly fit the beds in, thin walls with little to no soundproofing, tiny gardens; all built so close together. Cars plummet once purchased then level out but continue to decrease slowly. New properties also plummet once purchased contrary to popular belief about property, but once the rest of the market goes up they recover to what you paid for them, then start to progressively rise in value due to a long life utility (often many hundreds of years). After this initial drop *their % price growth will lag, and after say 5-10 years their value will be similar to the older 70s or 80s blocks in the street.*

*I have drawn a graph to show you what I mean. Lets say you buy a new build at £150,000. Depending on how well you bought it, the day after you buy it will likely be worth around 10%-15% less in value, say around £125,000. The value will probably stagnate for a further period of time even if the general market is rising. Eventually market rises will drag the value up, but only to the level of similar type/size properties in areas that were established around 15-20 years ago. In the example below, the existing property that was bought on an estate that had been built for 20 years cost £100,000. This is £50,000 cheaper than the new build was initially but after 15 years the value of the 2 properties have come together and become similar. The new build in the new area is now 20 years old and is valued along the same lines as other 20 year old properties. Why would you buy the new build if it is an investment?*

*I became fascinated by Car valuation/depreciation when trading cars and importing them from Ireland. My research had shown me that the majority of Car depreciation happened in years 1 and 2. For example a new BMW M3 I had in the 2011 was £65K new and became worth £40K within 12 months(!) Looking at it more closely, it was probably worth £50K the day after it left the forecourt. Virtually all 'new assets,' are worth considerably less as soon as purchased. Watches are the same, properties, computers, most Art, virtually everything. I found the three year old sweet spot in Cars, where you got the maximum benefit of depreciation, but could still get a modern car of the same generation/type. You could get away with small yearly drops in value that wouldn't hurt your pocket after the first three years, but still have a great Car that didn't cost too much to maintain. Property is similar, except one very powerful point: the general market in the background is often going up, pushing prices of neighbouring properties higher. Over a long enough period of* time this means that no matter how much above the market you paid for your new build, it will inevitably/eventually start to go up in value.

A simple graph below illustrates this point, you can see that just after year 3 on the X axis the curve gets a lot more shallow, meaning less depreciation for you if you buy at this point.

Between mid '06 and '07, I had bought a lot of existing houses, many on similar streets and in local suburbs. I had done a deal with Rob that we would go 50-50 on the deals; everything we bought was for the both of us. I would do all the buying and managing the investments, and put any necessary cash or expertise of 'no money down,' or 'none of our own money down,' in, and Rob would mentor me through his life coaching practice and take on future responsibilities in business together, that I'll share with you later. Rob also got me into running and exercise; we'd go out running around the new Hampton Estates at 6AM for one hour, and it raised my well-being and productivity levels to another stratosphere.

*(NOW) Productivity is very closely linked to energy, motivation and well-being. I never saw it in my former years, but drinking lots and general lethargy must have robbed me of 100's or 1,000's of hours of productive work. Rob came along and had black belts in martial arts, would run and go to the gym everyday, and once we started running together I learned where he got all his results-based energy from. Although this is not a health or personal development book, I must highly recommend exercise in your pursuit of wealth and business success. In fact, Will Smith, one of the most successful people on the planet, in more than one industry, with his super-success sperm that even gave his children success-star quality, says that his two secrets to success are 'running and reading.' I recommend you watch some of his inspirational videos.*

*Another valuable lesson at this point is in partnering or JV'ing (Joint Venturing). Rob and I are very different, and I can cite this as the main reason we are still in partnership nearly a decade later with successful enterprises We didn't really know the benefit of our differences when we started, but it is something we have carried forward and recommend to the tens of thousands of people we train at Progressive. People want to go into business with people like them, because we all relate to people with common interests, and this is often the worst thing you can do in business. If two of you in business do the same thing, one isn't needed. You'll both do the same things, getting in each others' way, and other important things that need doing that neither of you like/can do, will not get done. In addition, when you cut a 50-50 deal, many of the niggles, doubts and voices disappear, especially when brining opposing yet complimentary skill sets. In the early Progressive days I had the chance to buy properties with other partners, and Rob had the chance to continue to grow his Life Coaching business, but we agreed to either drop these avenues or cut each other in 50-50. To this day this is the best deal we have done and it means I no longer have to question all those things I used to when getting into deals and business with others.*

## *Real* value

The great benefit of buying older existing properties is that you can (much more accurately) ascertain the *real* value. You can drive around the areas and find common stock, you can speak to Agents to get exact and recent sold prices, and you can trawl Land Registry for the history of sales on the same street; something totally impossible with new, overseas or off plan properties, because nothing else had been built like it. There are/were no comps. I much preferred having a more proven and accurate valuation model, and felt like any equity was real as opposed to 'paper.'

My early years at home in Surabaya.

Mark and Rob with Lord Sugar at the 2011 Progressive Property SuperConference

Mark with Bob Geldof at the 2012 Progressive Property SuperConference

Mark and Rob with James Caan at the 2010 Progressive Property SuperConference

Mark with Frank Bruno at the 2013 Progressive Property SuperConference

Mark with Karren Brady at the 2013 Progressive Property SuperConference

You can go and could learn the local rental market quite quickly, as anyone can, and certainly light years quicker than one on the other side of the planet. It didn't take long to learn which streets were good investments and which streets were bad, and I could funnel all my investments (by this time over 20 properties) though one Letting Agent who had been tested against others locally. Using one Letting Agent, one refurb team, one plumber, one electrician and so on creates efficiencies that save valuable time and money. I can quickly influence the return on my investments through cost savings, local management knowledge, accurate price perception. This is impossible when you are too far away because there are way too many variables and management is totally out of your control.

*(NOW) Property management, although boring for many dreamy investors, is where much of the money is made or lost. The buying is the (relatively) easy part. Management is probably the most important part of owning a property, and the work or results only really coming once management kicks in, not by celebrating your huge discounts then lighting your Cigar. If rent does not come in frequently, timely and continually, you will be covering the mortgage with your salary or worse, credit, and the profit will be negative. Tenant selection is vital; get this wrong and you'll have months of no rental payments, court proceedings and huge refurbs every two or three years; all of which turns your profit into a net loss. Maintenance costs need to be controlled by you or your managers, or contractors will happily go and spend all your money on things of no capital value whatsoever. The closer your assets are to you, the more you or managers can keep control of this, and have your net profit flowing in each month.*

The more Rob and I were buying for ourselves locally, the more this gave me the itch that the deals Chris wanted me to sell were not as good as the ones I was buying. I didn't want to sell deals to investors that I didn't think were right for them, and I was now finding undeniable proof through my parallel testing. Chris was becoming increasingly forceful over the sale of some of his more dubious schemes. He had sniffed that Rob and I had become resistant to these deals, and that we'd brush his mood swings under the carpet and sell what we wanted (UK based), and he got more agitated and suspicious. By now, Rob and I were going out socialising, going to networking events together, even sitting desk to desk at the other end of the office from Chris, and this alliance we formed, that didn't include him, turned him wildly mad. He'd throw accusations around about us wanting to leave and set up in direct competition, and that we were out buying for ourselves through local Estate Agents. Although nothing wrong with buying our own deals (we had no contracts with Chris and had tried to include him), Chris was losing control and this made him angry. And his paranoia was becoming a reality.

Things really began to spiral when Rob did a big presentation in front of 200 people at an event one of Chris's contacts had organised. It was Rob's first major talk, and although good considering his lack of experience, Rob didn't stick to the topics Chris wanted. Rob also slipped out on stage that we had bought 11 properties together (Rob has a habit of saying what he thinks before thinking what he says, especially on stage). Chris went totally berserk, shouting 'I KNEW it, I KNEW it. You do NOT buy deals like that, you ONLY buy deals through Acorn.' He lambasted me all the way home and before we got back to Peterborough he had imposed a worldwide ban on us buying local properties.

The next morning Chris called a meeting. Furious about how the presentation had gone, he announced in the office in front of everyone that Rob was 'shit,' and that we have a new presenter. He then waited for our reaction, and when we didn't say anything, he exclaimed 'it's

ME!' I think I sniggered at this point and realised that within a few hours this would change when it dawned on Chris that he could barely sell a packet of nuts off stage without bullying. The reality was that he was angry and looking for people to blame. He didn't have the courage or work ethic to stand on stage and do the presentations. He was looking to gain more control, and he knew he was losing it. The more he did this, the further away it pushed us.

I can't profess to be an innocent bystander in all of this, because some of Chris's fears were justified. We had indeed been talking about leaving for a while before we did, and how we could run our own company. Of course we innocently, perhaps naively thought we could do it much better than Chris, and felt we were doing it anyway, it was just that Chris's cheques were bigger than ours. Rob was chomping at the bit to set up a new company and would have left the day after he started, but I didn't feel like the time was right. I wanted a little more security. Rob would keep saying the time will never be right and would make all these plans on his windows mobile phone of everything we needed to set up our own business. As much as I really wanted to do it, I just let him crack on because there was always my Dad's voice in my head about risk.

## 'Chris's' new model

The penultimate nail in the coffin was when Chris finally announced that existing property was worth looking at, and that he thinks we should sell it! Finally, after 18 months! We had been doing diligence on an existing buying model that seemed to be operating successfully, and spent a considerable amount of our spare time working out the intricacies, so that we could take it to Chris in what would be a last chance effort at making things work at Acorn. In true Chris style, after we approached him, he called a meeting down the Drapers Arms to set up our new business with Rob and I and another of our investors, Mark (the office managers' husband). Mark had become Chris's latest project since he had shown some interest in selling. He took us to a sticky, dingy Beer-pungent cubicle, and as was always the case with 'Chris's' new business ideas, the whole structure was devised on a Weatherspoon's napkin or Beermat. After no more than 3 minutes discussing the model and sales strategy, Chris bulldozed in and announced how the shares of this new company would be allocated. 'Mark (me), you can have 20%, Mark, you're getting 20%, Rob you can have 5% and I'll have 55%, right that's the deal done let's all shake on it NOW.'

This pushed me right over the edge and the fact that I didn't care about these behaviours anymore now proved to me that I had to leave with Rob. I could see in Rob's face that although he was trying to smile, he wanted to shove the napkin where the sun never shines and for Chris to smoke it. But one of the things that was holding me to Acorn was the £15K in share money I'd given Chris. However, by now I'd earned well at Acorn, learned even more, and so I was getting closer to accepting the write off of the capital in my mind. Despite all Chris's mannerisms and my recollection of events, we had some good funny moments when he was on his post Coffee high, and I was grateful for the opportunity to learn. Chris had introduced me to some good investing models, some interesting people, of course Rob, and every Friday he'd force us to down tools and watch 'The Secret,' with him before an early finish to the Draper's Arms. I didn't want to leave in an abrasive manner, so the timing and circumstance was very important to me. However Rob made sure we put a massive Spanner in all of that :-)

## Value in Local(ity) Summary

Many hundreds of thousands starting out, got suckered right in by those big, colourful, lifestyle brochures and dreamy holiday & new build homes. This, as we learned the hard way, is vanity. It's emotional buying. Buying local enables you to have a better understanding of tenant demand, actual sale price, who the local surveyors are, best and worst. Estate and Letting Agents, refurbishment teams, solicitors, competitors to keep close, actual achievable rentals, best streets with highest uplift potential, and so on. Buy as locally to you, or within a tight Geographical area as possible. There are Goldmine areas all over the country, even in London, from top to bottom.

# 11. Lessons from the end to the beginning

By now our plans to leave were cementing. Rob had started to talk to a marketer who we will call Bob who could 'fill rooms', and we'd decided on our model, that (importantly) we really believed in. Rob had put together some detailed planning documents, right down to how many chairs, desks and computers we'd need for the new business. Rob even detailed what staff we would need to 'borrow', from Acorn for a few years, and noted them down, all on his windows mobile phone. Rob had been on a trip to Australia learning how to become a life coach and public speaker, funded by Chris, who felt that Rob owed him for that. He thought he was creating multiple income streams by introducing Rob to life coaching and public speaking, and that he owned Rob even more. This was much a exercise of control on Rob as it was to benefit the business.

As our plans to leave progressed, Rob then went off on a reality TV show to film him coaching in a locked away house, kind of like Big Brother but with a positive outcome. Chris thought this would propel Acorn onto the NATIONAL stage.

The reality was that it wasn't really that relevant and didn't make any difference to the business. We had set a date to leave Acorn by this point and whilst Rob was away filming (for around 3 weeks) I had already cleared my desk and computer, and was mentally preparing myself to deliver the news to Chris on Rob's return. Rob was relishing the standoff opportunity and to deliver his resignation personally. I didn't want any confrontation and the ensuing predictable Volcanic eruption.

A couple of days before Rob was due to return, Chris came in one morning with a strange demeanour: I knew something was wrong. He wasn't his usual belligerent, coffee fuelled self. Chris was not able to control or hide his emotions very well, and approached me and said: 'Right, I've been told by a good source that Bob told him you're planning to leave and set up in DIIIIIIRECT competition with Acorn.' I didn't really know how to react and I wasn't ready to be confronted, and Rob wasn't there, so I denied it. Chris left me another couple of hours acting very strangely all morning and into the afternoon. He was totally out of his routine, and was even wearing different clothing. I could see him trying to take control of the other staff; people that we had a relationship with because he was never there. He was pulling them into private one to one meetings in a hush hush manner, and it was clear through the glass that he was preparing for a confrontation: rallying his troops to take his side and a last stand against us.

I took the earliest opportunity to leave Rob a voicemail message that the Cat was out of the bag, but he couldn't take calls whilst on set. Chris approached me again that afternoon, having stored up all his anger, and pointed at me ferociously, 'RIGHT, I've decided that you're sacked and you can phone Rob and tell him he's fired. Clear your desk and go nnnnnnnNOW.' So I scurried some papers and my phone and left.

I had a personal deal bought through Acorn going on with a developer at this time, and rang him to check that the deal was still on track as soon as I walked out of the office. It was clear that Chris had been on the phone to the lady on the sales desk, trying to put them off selling it to me. She had gone from positive and receptive to extremely cold. Chris was on a personal crusade to call everyone and bully them into believing we were the Anti-Acorn-Christ. He was fully committed to slander and blacken our names. I managed to get the deal completed, much to the disgust of Chris, I later discovered on the grapevine.

I called Rob again, still not being able to get through. I text him to call me urgently once he had the chance. He called me back and I delivered the news sheepishly, yet weirdly to me he found it exciting, somewhat amusing and as he called it 'an opportunistic blessing in disguise,' but I was not as amused as Rob. I was concerned about the money I had invested, Chris's mission to slander us and the uncertain future ahead. I was being paid well, and that had just come to an abrupt end. I chewed my hands for a few days restlessly until Rob returned.

Upon Rob's return and on the first chance we had, we went to see Chris at Acorn to try to smooth things over, and talk about a parting of ways that was reasonable (and in keeping with UK employment law). He'd already changed the locks on the doors, and when we went in all the staff, many our friends, acted cold. He immediately sent us away and told us to come back later at a time set by him. He wanted the meeting in the office, which surprised us as it would be in front of the other staff. I was highly suspicious of why he'd want to hold the meeting in full view and earshot of so many people, and thought he had some kind of plan or ulterior motive, true to Chris's devious nature. Why would he have what was likely to be an emotionally charged riot in earshot of the rest of the team?

We came back under orders and sat down at the meeting table fully prepared to cut a fair and reasonable deal with Chris. Although both of us held some resentment, we didn't want undue conflict. After all, we'd been fired (without following any employment protocol). We had a strong case for wrongful and unfair dismissal, but had zero intention of going down this road, we just wanted a fair break. Rob even said he'd forego some of his commissions owed, and reading now it would have been pretty hypocritical considering my attitude to employees and tribunals having now seen both sides. I had quite a weak negotiating position and would have been ripe for an easy deal to cut us loose that would have benefitted Chris more than us. But as soon as commissions owed to Rob (in the region of £10,000) were broached, and my £15,000 share money, Chris threw his hands all over the place, leaning back on two legs of his chair and banging the glass desk, repeatedly shouting, 'You'll get NNNNNNOTHING! You'll get NOTHING from me, ever.' The meeting turned into a full on shouting match. It was like Rob had held in a years worth of abuse and let it fly once Chris gave him the chance. I was sat between two people breathing fire at each other. I thought Rob was going to pull some martial arts moves on Chris, and that Chris was going to get a Tazer out. No one knew where to look, and Chris's designer, pretending not to look, was taking notes under the table. I found this strange. Mike, Chris's friend who owned the furniture shop below, ran up and told us all to shut up as he had customers downstairs. Steam continued to fly out of Chris's ears and nostrils and the rage kept flowing.

With adrenaline-stench in the air, I felt very angry and wronged that we'd been kicked out without any of our commissions due and my capital disappearing into Chris's Paul Smith fund. I felt like I'd lost £15,000 and my shares in the company, which should have been worth a lot more now, and I knew Chris would do me out of these in one way or another. It was all downward spiraling. A few days later a very aggressive letter arrived from an employment lawyer laying out Chris's case which was riddled with lies. This filled us with a sense of wrong doing, and aggressive commitment to fight for what we thought was right. At that moment I decided I would put my money into dealing with him. All the bullying, lies and mental abuse boiled over and I wanted him dealt with.

*(NOW) Before I continue in the aftermath of Acorn, there were many valuable lessons I gained on the front line, as a foot soldier that have laid the foundations for successful investing and businesses. I could write a 'how no to' manual based on my observations at Acorn, many of them saving me immediate expense and some I wasn't ready for yet, but would store in the locker:*

## 1. The best education is on the front line.

*Courses are great, a formal education can be of benefit for specialised subjects, reading and studying give you a good starting block, but there is no substitute for actual real experience. But there are varying degrees of experience, and the front line method of getting real hands on 'work-experience,' has been the best kind in my life. In the world of business and investing this is relatively easy to do, but it is also just as easy not to do and so most people don't do it. You simply find a company like Progressive, or a Letting or Estate Agent, or Acorn back then like I did who are in the business you want to be in, and you ask for work. This work could be paid, it could be free, it doesn't have to be long term; it doesn't really matter because the money is not the main benefit; the front-line education holds most of the value. In the grand scheme it will be a relatively low cost route to your high life compared to traditional routes or expensive mistakes*

*If you choose a big corporate machine for this you'll learn about systems and processes, an education we never had, but more because of what you can't find out than what you can. If you go for an Entrepreneurial set up/start up like Acorn, you'll get right into the inner workings of every facet, but it will be a little more haphazard, there will be bad habits that you'll have to figure out for yourself, and it will be less professional. Make your choice, but I feel like my front-line education was accelerated into hyper-drive because of the unique situation at Acorn.*

## 2. Management: 'how not to'

*I will be detailing this later, but the over-riding lesson is that the effective management of staff is your, the business owners,' responsibility. It is all too easy to blame people for non performance, but what I really learned at Acorn was that in nearly every case it is down to the owner/manager hiring the wrong person in the first place, or someone who was good but in a different/wrong role, or not taking responsibility to train or induct someone properly, and/or managing them emotionally (badly). If you invest time in your staff assets, training them properly, making them feel important, never berating through the learning phase or in public, giving responsibility, fair and consistent treatment and a clear career and personal development progression plan, you'll build a great team. They will continue building downwards for you carrying your values and developing a large scale business on your behalf. They will work hard for you because they feel valued. They will be far more likely to stay for the long term, be loyal to you and never feel the need to turn their back on you.*

*Great managers control their emotions, staying professional and discreet at all times. I saw how Rob reacted to being called 'shit,' in front of all of us when he had worked so hard to train as a speaker, and I knew how it caused resentment and embarrassment. A great manager is as fair as they can be, and does their best to motivate with incentives, rewards, compliments and progression and further responsibility opportunities. I don't profess to be the best manager in the world, in fact many Entrepreneurs are bad managers, but I gained valuable 'how not to,' experience through Chris.*

### 3. Staff leaving

*Rob and I were proud of our record of no staff leaving after two years of running Progressive, then 4 left in revolt and unison to set up in competition directly against us. Watching Chris at my time at Acorn, he had various business partners, staff (not just Rob and I), all of whom left quickly. Sure, staff leaving or setting up in competition is part and parcel of growth if you're in business long enough, but if you follow step 2. you'll keep it to an absolute minimum, or if people have the hunger to leave and/or grow, they'll approach you before 'going behind your back,' giving you the opportunity to progress them.*

## 4. Competition

*Competition is essential for your accelerated growth and commitment to the cause. Chris thought that 'all competition are Baaaaaastards!' This is over simplistic. Through Acorn I certainly experienced the over obsessive, unhealthy competitive feeling, which can cause ill feeling, ill health and unhappiness. I would not recommend getting so obsessed with beating competition that it rules your life, thus taking you away from your main aims and vision, but for sure monitor, study and spy on competition to stay grounded and quickly reactive in your industry. View competition as a blessing to keep you focused and motivated and don't let them rule/ruin your life.*

## 5. Only spend on income generating assets

*Had Chris preserved capital (detailed later), he may have been able to ride out the harder times. The reality was he spent it all, and much of it before the service that had been paid for was delivered, so he was always very exposed to any small change in markets or regulations. Be very strict on the difference between spending and investing, limit spending on depreciating liabilities to an absolute minimum, and invest only/mostly in assets that appreciate in value and over the long term. Have cash and assets to protect against future changes and 'irregular shocks.'*

## 6. Offer good long-term products

*Whilst a good 'snake oil,' salesman, Chris couldn't sell anything with sustainability because it wasn't exciting enough (in his view), and none of it ever lasted long enough. There will be a myriad of fads and next big things that find their way to your door as you open for business, most of which don't work and even more not relevant to your vision. This will also increase your costs to a higher life of luxury due to mistakes, brand damage and the initial, expensive start up cost of continually starting again. You should create products and services that have sustainable value, and can be sold over many years or decades, that people need and desire. The higher the lifetime value, the less affected by market variations your businesses will be, and the less you will have to spend on repetitive research and development, and the constant starting again that takes all the time. You also create 'mind space,' brand with longevity and history of sales, and you become the 'go to,' person or company for it. This deep level of awareness means you sell when you are closed and asleep, triggering buying decisions simply in the thoughts of your customers. If you think of a fizzy drink or a pair of trainers, the common brands that first come to mind owns that space and is selling inside your mind. Very powerful indeed. And very much long term thinking and strategy that compounds positively the longer you are in it.*

## 7. Give great service

*Chris was actually good at getting customers excited in short term gains, but this was in reality an expensive illusion. Anyone can fool customers in the short term, but not the long term; water finds its own level. Nothing compares in business to great service and customer experience, and it will outweigh and outlast any big promise, unrealistic benefit or instant dream. Of course, we have let the odd customer down in the past and we all strive for a somewhat unattainable perfection, but if ever we've had client issues they are nearly always solved by picking up the phone, apologising proactively, being nice, listening and then improving your product or service based on their feedback.*

## 8. Take your time over big, strategic decisions

*Chris's decision making was dependent on his caffeine-fix curve, and at any lag in the curve the decisions were nearly always bad. Impetuosity and reactivity will cost significant time and financial sums. Later I discuss*

'Inaction,' and the power and benefit of taking your time over important decisions or 'sitting on your hands,' to ride out volatile markets. Sometimes actively not acting is best.

## 9. Make every £ spent on marketing count

We saw Chris project his pressure onto us when a £1,200 adwords spend brought in nine leads, not including paying the consultant who generated them. Close them or you're fired,' was a frequent order. His money wasting antics extended from capital to marketing expenses, and it drummed into us, especially Rob, that you want to get maximum value for every marketing £ spent. Our favoured method is known as 'direct marketing.' Direct marketing measures the £ return on the £ spend, for the initial outlay, and the lifetime value. Never would you hear sacrilege in the direct marketing world of 'brand awareness,' and 'PR baby,' you want to be able to test and measure every £ spent and the return it generates. In the first 2 years of Progressive Rob was getting clients who had a lifetime value of upwards of £30,000 for sometimes less than a pound, and always less than £3 for a 'lead.' These figures vary across industries and the CPL (cost per lead) in industries changes over time, but you have to waste a lot of these '£3 per leads,' to not make profit, especially on high ticket items you may be selling. I love the measurable nature of direct response marketing and the ease at which you can calculate exactly the return on each pound-prisoner, gaining maximum low cost benefit.

## 10. Processes & systems (for everything)

One of the most stark differences between Acorn and a corporate enterprise was the (lack of) systems and processes. In a large corporate enterprise or franchise, virtually every action will have a documented process within a manual of operations. There will be a clear and correct way for every stage of the procedure, making it 'child's-play' easy to create consistent experience with minimal cost of training and staffing. New employees or non specialist staff can get quickly up to speed and create the same experience the MD could.

At Acorn, there wasn't a single process. Inconsistency was the order of the day, and we did random things at random times based on how Chris felt at that given time. You wouldn't know what, where, why or how you were doing anything, because there was no set or right way to perform any task. To be expected and demanded to get the result without the how to do it is insanity. And then to keep changing it is even worse. It would, ironically, have saved so much of Chris's ongoing time if he had documented all the right actions and created a manual that other staff could follow. It's also not that difficult and can be done 'on the job,' as you go through the pain barrier of doing it yourself in the early days. Despite this valuable lesson, and the pain we felt with Chris' incessant inconsistencies, it still took Rob and I nearly 2 years to start implementing our systems and processes properly because, like most small businesses, we got sucked into doing it all, proclaiming that we 'had no time,' to work 'on,' the business. We paid the price for this, as you'll learn later. Start systems and processes now while they're clear, easy and there aren't too many of them. Or, better still; hire a virtual assistant (VA) to do it for you on the job. It's easier than ever with audio recording apps, transcription and text reader apps, and centralised online file sharing systems.

Of course anyone who has any business and reads this will think, 'yes Mark, but the reality is not as easy.' People have often tried to hire/outsource or systemise, and it's not worked out, or they're so busy they don't have time to, or they hire someone wrong, or they go bad, or they set up in competition, etc. I have experienced all of these so I'm here to tell you this is normal. It is part of the journey and the process, much like gaining knowledge, losing some money while learning how to invest or injuries at the gym. So you have two choices:

1. Don't do it and stay comfortable where you are now

2. Do it, go through some bumps and challenges and get to your desired outcome

One of my favourite techniques to manage and maintain systems and processes is through 'random spot checking.' People are smart and they can second guess predictable movements, so the key to effective systems and management is to randomly make spot checks that are unannounced and unexpected. I don't think his technique needs long explanation; it just works because people/people operating processes know at anytime they could be tested or even caught out. Use a simple diary reminder system by reminding yourself every given period of time (make it recurring and have a secret name if other people can see your calendar).

## That Letter

The Lawyer's letter was the straw that broke the Camel's back. It was Chris's last stab at controlling us, and typically brutal in nature. It was as though somehow he'd got a Lawyer to write a legal letter (which Chris didn't understand) yet influenced by him. I could just picture the Lawyer writing it and Chris moving him over and adding bits in himself, 'Yes, that'll get those Baaaaaaaastards!'

(As a side note, 'Those Baaaaaastards,' was Chris's stock phase for anyone who didn't bend to his will. It still makes me chuckle to this very day, as most of the people who've ever met Chris would end up on his 'those Baaaaaaastards' list).

That letter demanded that all 'cuuumpany property', be returned immediately, including the Laptop Rob had, and threatened legal action if we set up a competing company. Of course it is fair and standard that reasonable non-competition rules are parts of employment contracts, so fair competition restrictions weren't our issue, despite the fact that we never had a contract at Acorn. We knew that to Chris that non-competition meant starve for a millennium and die starve slowly in terrible, skeletal pain. Perhaps I was naïve of this back then, but employing many people now, it is just standard business practice to have fair and reasonable non competitive contracts/clauses. The thing is, we never had any contracts with Chris or Acorn, and any kind of process or agreement would have meant Chris would have run out of napkins. So to post-impose unreasonable and unenforceable anti competitive restrictions was ludicrous, and made us even more vigilant in the setting up of Progressive and the defence of these futile methods of control. Our new business would be significantly different from his also with a different type of customer which made the letter even more ridiculous. Ironically, the new business venture we were moving into we'd offered to Chris, and this was important for our conscience to feel that we'd done the wrong thing. If Chris had been amenable, it's likely that I (less likely Rob) could have stayed at Acorn. Though it would have cost me many millions in not running my own business enterprises. A high (opportunity) cost that would have been.

We needed to take advice because we weren't well versed in law and this letter was so aggressive it simply forced us to see a Lawyer. From Chris's point of view this was counter-productive, but the Lawyer must have been rubbing his hands for the £15,000 fees about to roll his way in a good old fashioned and well-engineered tribunal-scrap. We spoke to a Lawyer who managed to hook us in nicely, listing out many areas in which Chris had contravened employment law, alluring our belief that we had a great case and had been truly wronged. Our case for getting back share and commission monies weren't as strong, but all in all we had a great case for wrongful and unfair dismissal, and so it all started. We weren't actually bothered in the slightest about wrongful or unfair dismissal despite how it was delivered; we'd have just walked right out without a fight and set up our business. However this was the only way we could recover funds that any reasonable employer would have legally paid, even if it was negotiated down.

Chris had made an illegal deduction of wages, and upon our reply this was paid very quickly. Once the laptop had been returned and a couple of letters back and forth, Chris took it upon himself to discredit us as his strategy for successfully defending our counter claims of wrongful and unfair dismissal. Chris had the computers forensically analysed and found salacious photographs of Rob with his girlfriend in a 'compromising position,' downloaded from his personal phone. Wholly irrelevant but blackmail nonetheless, but more damning was Rob's detailed master plan for the new business including the new inventory and new staff members we were looking to employ(!).

Looking back at this, I find it all highly amusing. At the time Rob was footloose and fancy free, and perhaps more careless than I'd have been. Rob seems to have more careless abandon than me, but I guess he didn't have a father like I did. The underlying issue here though was much stronger. Chris had taken personal property of Rob's that had zero relevance to the case, and was attempting to use it as blackmail. I remember him sending the pictures through in a brown envelope and it reminded me of some kind of US police TV show, and totally in keeping with Chris's tactics. Our solicitor didn't think it was relevant but she (our Lawyer) and Rob (who didn't seem worried in the slightest) found it all very funny.

Things were getting messy now, and I felt that Chris would start resorting to less conventional tactics that he probably had experience from in his Police days, so I went to see a private investigator. He found the whole case hilarious and gave us a few ideas. Around the same time one of Chris's employees (who shall remain nameless), who was still in contact with us and very much felt the same way towards Chris as we did, let us in on the misdemeanors at Acorn. As usual Chris had been out having philandering rendezvous with other women, despite being in a 'serious,' relationship, at least to his partner. An employee told us of one in particular who he had been seeing more frequently. As is usually the case, her husband found out what was going on and in a rage decided to make his way down to the Acorn office. As he arrived at the office in the evening he was spotted outside looking angry and preparing himself for his 'meeting' with Chris. Being much bigger then Chris he looked like a weight trainer who had just popped some steroids. As Chris realised who he was his demeanour changed, cowering behind the intercom system as the well built husband demanded to see him. Chris' usually dictatorial voice dropped to a squeak and he kept repeating 'no violence, no violence!' Luckily for Chris the front door and door opening system on his newly built office was solid and the man eventually left.

Using the private investigators advice I decided to write to Chris as still the only other remaining shareholder of the company, asking him to provide answers pertaining to this incident. I also questioned whether the safety of the employees had been compromised by the aggressor, and if and how the incident had been logged by the office manager at the time, who happened to be Chris's girlfriend, and if not, why not. I never heard back from him on this manner.

I set these letters up as a series of counter attacking defence, and he'd receive one every two weeks or so. We were also tipped off that he would take trips to Panama, often taking staff members on jollies, using company money, so I included this in the correspondence. The whole legal episode culminated in a showdown at the local employment tribunal within which we'd hired a Barrister, who predictably made Chris's evidence look ridiculous. Having been a Police officer, we thought he would have performed a little better on the stand, but his compulsive lies and stock phrases such as 'I know because I wrote it in my pocket book,' were picked apart with ease. Chris had clearly forced a couple of the other staff to lie for him. We were very angry about this but it was a stark lesson from our first (and only) experience in an employment tribunal.

Rob and I felt good about the experience in the tribunal. We stuck to the facts of the case, Rob did well to control his emotions and I felt that we'd been honest when questioned. Of course Chris may beg to differ, but we remained credible and it became clear we would easily win the case. Chris' side of the story might be hard to get as he has since fled to European havens having been chased by various creditors. In fact I didn't really need to change his name for this book because he has done that himself.

Having made a couple of offendingly-low offers to settle, Chris ended up offering us £15,000 just before the last hearing. We ended up settling on the steps just before the hearing started. Although we felt fantastic about winning, the vindication of the events, the clearing of our names that Chris tried so hard to tarnish, and the outing of what we believed was the truth, our legal bill came in at a similar number as our settlement. This was another lesson in who is usually victorious in these exchanges, and it wasn't us. It was satisfactory to know that Chris's legal bill must have been the same, if not more, plus the costs he'd have to pay, so it would stand him double-down at around £30,000. I don't usually feel vindictive towards anyone as it is counter-productive, but I needed to feel a sense of justice after all that I'd been through, and the customers and those around him who lost out. More importantly we could put to bed the emotional turmoil it caused, which all in all lasted nearly two years, and have the business protected so we could get on with making a fair and reasonable living.

If you want to experience the true low cost high life experience, I recommend staying out of court where possible.

## Lessons from the Tribunal

*(NOW) Looking back, and having been on both sides of the employment fence, it's vital to make the best effort you can when employing people to get along well, be consistent and fair, manage well with systems, processes and agreements, and remember it doesn't cost anything to deal with small issues as soon as they arise. If you have to let people go, let them go sympathetically and agreeably where possible. It is all too easy to get emotional and take personally what employees (and employers) do, and this all ends up costing you £1,000's. The Entrepreneur or small business owner can't afford to get unfairly treated by employees, but it costs more to go through a tribunal with them. I've found that as you grow your business and become less personal and more detached from the fact that it's 'your baby,' this becomes easier. If I could turn back time, I'd certainly be more logical and less emotional in these circumstances. Often senior execs are much better at dealing with HR issues who don't own their own company, because they are more detached.*

*The time and negative energy it takes in legal cases, often not to cover costs, is not just about the direct cost, but more about the opportunity cost of the time and energy that you could have put into a money making business or investment. Compounded over 20 years this dead time could have made £10,000's or more.*

*Be very clear about expectations and honesty around business partners and staff. Be clear on your expectations without bullying or upsetting people. Your job is to manage people's emotions. Don't ridicule people in front of others or make them feel or look stupid. Have clear agreements, contracts and processes to manage any disagreements early and clearly. be fair, honest and consistent, and you'll have permission to lead, challenge and grow your staff.*

*People only ever work for themselves, and never for you, even if they work 'for you.' You have to make sure that they are getting their needs met, and that you're helping them along their career path. As soon as they feel controlled or manipulated you'll lose them, and they'll turn and resist any growth of your company. They may go as far as to turn against you and put much time and energy into fighting you.*

*Surround yourself around people who have similar goals, objectives and vision. If the people you work or partner up with see things in a very different way, their paths will always be wildly different and cause conflict. It is your job to carefully scrutinize people's vision, motives and goals and make sure, while skillets can be different, that visions are similar. Regardless of how it all ended, it is obvious looking back that we were always going in a different path to Chris and Acorn. If we'd both seen this earlier perhaps some of the conflicts would have been avoided.*

*Don't just think twice; think ten times before instructing Lawyers to resolve conflict. You may be angry and/or emotional at the time, and these battles/Lawyers often provide a welcoming cathartic release, and to side with you to right the wrong that you feel the other party has inflicted upon you. The reality however is that financially it is often the case that you will be worse off. Clearly dependent on how much money is at stake vs. the Lawyers bill, it is important to remember that the proceeds from cases will often be more than outweighed by Lawyers bills. In our case at Acorn, the settlement was £15,000 and the total legal bills with* both sides added up were around triple the payout! It seems such a small and insignificant amount of money for the time and bad energy, looking back. Most friends I have in business have had many similar experiences. As many divorcing couples will tell you, the best settlements are negotiated by two parties willing to be reasonable, give a little and put their emotions to one side, before tribunal/court hearings.

During the dispute but before the settlement, Chris had dispatched a mutual friend/investor, Mick, to try and put the point that it would be the Lawyers who'd get all the money, so why don't you stop doing this? Whilst he was probably right in that the Lawyers made the most, looking back our primary motivation was what we saw as the justice that came from this process, even more than the financial settlement, and were therefore unwilling to listen. We'd possibly do the same again, but it might not be the best advice. We'd have almost certainly made more than £15,000 with the time given back to us to focus on our current business at that time.

The thing that hurt me the most through the entire Acorn tribunal process were the lies that were damaging our name, brand, reputation and sales of our new business. The biggest gain we had in the tribunal was the right and proof we had to protect and defend out names, this was more valuable than any money we received (to then give to our Lawyers). I don't believe in bullying in business, even when you have the control, but I do believe in vehemently and aggressively protecting your name and reputation from defamation, slander and lies. Treat your business reputation as you would your child and defend it to the end. Don't let people bully you.

## Sympathy for Chris?

As I've gained more experience in business, I have been able to see things from Chris's side and understand some of his reactions; employees and employers point of view. He must have found it hard running a business with all the cashflow challenges, VAT and payroll that every business has to face. We didn't understand why he'd be in a vicious mood every three month like a cycle, but huge VAT bills aren't exciting. Plus it was a relatively new venture for him that he wasn't experienced in, and we all have to start somewhere.

When we left, half of his work force and all the senior management of the company went in one stroke. From his point of view he could have felt that he put us together and introduced us into the world, which is partly true, and thus would feel that he gave us the opportunity that was now fuelling our own interests. Equally Rob and I would now have a major issue if our employees were planning to set up in a similar field. When you are in business long enough, it/this happens, and we have tasted this experience on more than one occasion. I am grateful that we were able to heed our own advice, stay emotionally detached and deal with these situations logically and fairly. Well most of them anyway.

Deep down I think Chris wanted to do the right thing, but he was plagued by his polarised and extreme emotions of over excitement or anger, and he brought this with him to work. Seeing situations from the other person's point of view keeps you grounded and realistic, and solves virtually all conflict. I believe he went from property to a haven in Cyprus after going bust in the UK, to being a hypnotist in Portugal. Although this comment could be seen as one-upmanship it certainly isn't. It is just evidence to the fact that if he'd stayed long term in property, he'd not have had to flee and be in businesses that aren't as lucrative. I now view all of this as positive experience and have exorcised any demons and would wish Chris well. He'd probably want to put me and Rob into a double headlock.

## Lessons from the end to the beginning - Summary

Systems are the backbone of any scalable businesses and portfolios. If you want to use leverage and have a portfolio that works for you, implement key models for systems after you've tested what works and what doesn't. Learn to do less yourself, and leverage and manage more. Work on your business more, and in the thick of it less. Avoid over control and learn to trust others. Build your team, get your message out there, nip small issues in the bud relatively quickly and monitor the KPI's of your business to constantly strive for the simplest route efficiency, providing a good service and making a profit. Have a vision that the world needs to hear, and you can profit handsomely while helping others too.

## 12. Progressive Progression

Before we left Acorn, plans were taking shape to set up a company together, mostly driven by a reaction to all the things we didn't want to do for/with Chris. It was certainly not going to be selling overseas, off plan, new build property or every latest scheme that was found on the depths of the webernet.

The chap that had told Chris that we were planning to defect, who was also talking to us about a Joint venture where he could 'fill rooms' (standard speak for him) for us to present our new property investing model to potential customers, had double crossed us. Chris took him on to do the same job as he was promising for us, but of course with much larger promises of a multi-millionaire lifestyle in six minutes. Bob had made many promises to us about our partnership, and this U-turn made us deeply annoyed, and even more focused on making Progressive a success. We now had an adversary to benchmark.

Once Progressive was set up, Chris focused a lot of his energy on our business rather than his. He had gone around the entire industry, telling everyone who would listen and everyone who wouldn't how we had planned 'to clear the office of all the equipment, take it all and set up in DIIIIIRECT competition to Acorn!' Other stories surfaced including Chris's discussions from some unsavoury characters planning to come and break our legs.

It is noteworthy that we didn't in any way see our business as competitive to Acorn. Of course I learned a lot at Acorn, but the models we were interested in building and selling at Progressive were anti-Acorn. In fact, the model we set up (now Progressive Portfolio Builder) and wrote a best-selling book about, was the one we had researched ourselves and given Chris the opportunity to take on at Acorn as a new venture. It was the 10% and 5% Chris would let us have that helped us make the decision to set up alone. We were to personally buy and offer to clients local, existing property that we would manage entirely for them, costing less and making more. Chris was sourcing worldwide properties for finder's fees with zero management and customer care.

Interestingly, a few months after we set up Progressive and word got out, and a short while after he bought his brand new £90,000 Aston Martin (that later got repossessed), Chris had set up the same model promising 'Armchair,' investments for clients. The small difference in the model was that we were offering a 5 property portfolio managed for a minimum of 6 years with generous 15% discounts, a fee of £5,000 per property and a working capital deposit pot to fund them, for the lifetime of the management term. Chris was offering a Million pound portfolio in one year all no money down without the need for deposits and with just a £50,000 fee to him.

(As I write this book now, sitting in Barbados with Rob typing for me, I just asked him: 'Where had he worked that model out?' Rob said, 'On the back of his last Napkin in the Drapers Arms!). Chris was certainly creative!

## Cost Control

To keep costs low at start up, we set up Progressive in Rob's 'dining room,' in his small two up two down house which was his first ever investment. My Mum became our PA, our first 'employee,' who worked for free to help us get started and to whom I am still very grateful to this day. She worked at Progressive for 6 great years. Thank you Mum! We bought second hand equipment, all the furniture from Ikea, used some of our existing equipment, and the set up costs were less than £1,500 for the whole business. We didn't pay ourselves a salary of any kind for many months. It hurt but it was necessary. William my step father kindly helped us with making sure the model worked and set about putting refurb procedures in place. He has an excellent mind when it comes to managing large scale projects for governments and organisations, delivering infrastructure projects such as the World Bank and the UN. He gave a lot of his time and for this I'm very grateful.

We worked very hard for the first few months, now that we were working for our own future. We went to as many networking, property and personal development events as we could get to (and afford) with a view to bringing in some clients for our business. It was graft at first. Despite having bought around twenty properties personally at this point, we were very new in business and people knew it, so we had to work much harder, be smarter with our brand, and find the right types of clients.

We quickly established clear and delineated roles. Rob had read the e-myth and we sat on our 2nd hand 'boardroom', table (a fold up job Rob had at home we made use of), and we followed the instructions in the book to the letter to set up our future 'org-chart.' I took all the property buying and management related roles, and Rob took all the marketing, sales and design ones. There were around ten future roles in the company of Progressive to make it ready in the future for exit or sale, and all had either 'Rob,' or 'Mark,' written in. I set about buying more properties for us personally and for the new clients Rob would find. Rob built the website, got started with our first book and found clients in our 'marketing department.'

*(NOW) I remember looking at this 'org chart,' with ten employees in it thinking 'that will take years to get to. 10 staff it a lot.' I wasn't even sure if I believed it, but went along with the process because it seemed like the right*

*thing to do. It's fun looking back as that seems so small now. It was a great lesson in setting both your goals and grand vision for what you want your business or life to look like.*

While Bob was 'filling rooms,' for Acorn, and people were going in a mad frenzy for his '£million no money down portfolio,' that he had a hired-gun saleswoman called Marie to sell for him (who'd sold all manner of off plan, overseas and such ventures that had turned to dust), we were struggling to get any business at all. We didn't have a database, we didn't have much experience on our own, we couldn't 'fill rooms,' and we didn't have any brand or history. For the first 6 months at least we had no income and it made me feel exposed. I really cut back on any spending I was doing personally, and I didn't enjoy all the voices in my head questioning if this would actually work, would people actually believe Chris's warped version of events and what he was saying about us, and how we would get clients in our makeshift office and Tumbleweed set up? Thankfully, at the height of these thoughts, things started to get good.

## Progressive Growth

Over time, but much quicker than I expected (probably the best part of a year), we steadily built our assets: website, brand, our 1st book, a handful of clients as proof, twenty through to thirty and then to fifty deals we'd bought for ourselves, a small but well nurtured database and some credibility with peers in the marketplace. Many people have said that Progressive had a meteoric rise, but I would say it was more 'Progressive.' In the same time at Acorn with Bob's database, Chris was masterminding his biggest scheme to date, 'going naaaaaaaational,' and putting 'Acorn on the map.' In fairness, Bob was pretty good at his part of the deal and he was filling rooms for Chris. The presenter, Marie, had experience selling properties for other companies, and of course selling

Chris's new product was going to be very easy for her to offer with the huge promise. But the wheels all started to fall off when the sales were coming in, but the delivery was not.

We met mortgage brokers and other networks who were telling stories of Chris's ramshackle organisation. I knew what it would take to be able to buy five to ten properties per client in a year: a God-inspired miracle. I knew what it would take to do all of these deals no money down: a God-inspired miracle. I knew what it would take to source and manage all these contacts and properties and clients all across the UK: a God-inspired miracle. In the first year when we had a handful of clients, I guess we'd bought around twenty properties, in that same year we heard that Chris and Bob pulled in around fifty clients, therefore building a need for a minimum of 250 properties to deliver on the promise. Yet in the time before Acorn went bust, they had bought only a handful (less than ten) for their clients, we we're told.

The stories kept flowing in from all sources. In the time they were supposed to be buying 250 properties for clients, not including setting up all the contacts, networks, buying infrastructure and management, they were having the time of their lives. There were 'buying trips' to Panama & Cyprus where Bob and Chris would get drunk with the clients and fight with each other. Two of his most senior employees allegedly 'drew parts of the male anatomy with shaving foam,' all over Chris' French doors in a drunken frenzy, and when Chris found out got one in a headlock and was 'peanutting,' his head in front of prospective clients. One night on this customer buying trip, Chris found some call girls in Cyprus, bought them back with one of his employees and had a night to remember. When some of the clients found out you can imagine them writing a cheque there and then for at lest two of their £Million portfolios?!

The Aston Martin had plummeted by around £40,000 by this point in time (two minutes research on Auto Trader told me).

More of these funds were invested in a Racehorse from one of his buying trips to Panama. Apparently some sort of 'huuuuge Spanish thoroughbred,' Chris thought it better to tell Bob (who was now a pseudo shareholder) that he had 'adopted,' a Racehorse 'out of the kindness of his heart.' What was even funnier was that it happened to be of the type which Chris's girlfriend rode…And it mysteriously found its way back to Europe shortly afterwards. The reality was that this Horse was for his girlfriend, which of course created a solid and trusting environment with his partner and staff, who viewed this as diverting money away from them.

*(NOW) It could be perceived that I write this with a certain amount of sour grapes. I must admit to being annoyed all through this time that we had an agreement with Bob, but I recount these events for you not just for amusement or out of spite, but for the serious lessons that lie within. This gratuitous spending of money is what puts most companies under. Chris would not be the first and won't be the last. So many companies run out of cash, and it is so important, especially in the early days, to protect it, saving every pound you can. Only spend on essential items, and get used or already depreciated non-assets where possible. 'Every pound is a prisoner.' Chris was like a cartoon version of how not to spend money in a company, all made worse by the fact that he couldn't deliver his product.*

*I also watched Acorn grow at its fastest rate in the year we left. In the early days that must have felt great for Chris, vindicating our departure, but the growth was unsustainable and he didn't have the foundations, systems, staff or experience to deliver at the same rate that he grew. It was like watching a tidal wave come in from the horizon, building momentum, and the huge crash was always inevitable. I'm sure as you read this you're not going to turn away opportunities to bring in a large volume of sales, but growth that is too fast can create huge delivery and reputational issues that will hurt or kill the long term-ism of your business. Rob and I saw this with many companies through the growth and recession of the mid to late 2000's, and in almost all the cases there simply were not enough cash reserves to sustain these businesses through leaner times. Conserve and protect cash at all costs, especially when times are good because they can reverse very quickly. I'll talk in detail about 'cash preservation' later.*

It was only a matter of time before Acorn would implode. He managed to drag it out for a couple of years, and we were surprised that it went that long, making every pop he could at us along the way; something he never seemed to fully let go of. Predictably in the end Acorn went into administration. Once the marketing tap shuts, there is no new money. Bob jumped ship just before it all went bang, and the committee that the clients had put together to chase Chris for their money had grown strength. Chris wriggled through the administration as much as he could and fled to Cyprus, leaving everything behind. He got into a few new schemes until he changed his name, moved to another Southern European country where I understand he now works as a stage hypnotist!

*(NOW) The best place to sort your problems out is right where you made them. Granted, Chris upset a lot of people, but he could have stayed to sort the issue out, and would probably have a good business now if he'd found the right people to help him, treated them well, and stayed on one thing long enough and for the long term.*

And to finally put the chapter and verse of Acorn to bed, one of the guys on the inside at Acorn, connected with Chris, put me in touch with the administrator. I found over £30,000 worth of stock, equipment, computer and telephone systems, designer furniture, interactive projector, orthopedic office chairs, expensive filing systems and more that was being liquidated from Acorn. I made a farcically low offer of £2,000 for the entire stock, and we settled at £2,400. We furnished our entire second (new) office when we moved out of Rob's house, with all this stock and had a Boutique London style office interior thanks to Chris's spending habits. This is low cost high life strategy implementation at its best. Rob still sits on his office chair today with an occasional smile. Of course I tell you this for the value/cost ratio and nothing at all to do with gloating or last laughs!

Ultimately, it was Chris 'high cost, high life,' where he lead a transient, short lived 'unaffordable life of luxury,' that was the end of his business and wealth.

## Lessons from the hardest year

Once Progressive passed it's 1st birthday and a lot of the hard work had been done, we now had a significant personal portfolio, and we had a real business; the two things in life I wanted the most. If I were to look back and, as I frequently get asked, 'do it differently,' here's what I would do if I had the time again, using the 'low cost, high life,' maxim:

### 1. Staff

I am about to break the 'low cost high life,' mantra here, a little like my father invested money in my private education despite hating spending any money. Hire in the best staff you can find earlier than you plan and can budget for. If you hire low cost staff, you get low cost work, and people are absolutely far and away the best investment you have in your business. People hire people because they are like them or they like them, but this is a mistake. Hire the right people, traits and skills for the specific role, and build a varied, broad ranging skill set power team. Hire people for the long term. Because it is a new business, hire the best who have experience and proven track record in the role you are hiring for. Most small business owners would say they can't afford to do that, but that's what keeps them small. When hiring you get a free month upfront, then you only have to pay them one twelfth of their annual salary, and the process starts over again. It is nowhere near the risk people think it is. As much as many deluded laptop Entrepreneurs think they can, you can't build a business on your own.

If you have clear Job Descriptions, Key Performance Indicators and Minimum Standards of Performance, and you train and induct your staff members well, managing them effectively, they will pay for themselves many times over, even if they're not in a direct sales role, and even if at first it is simply by freeing you to focus on sales and marketing activities. If it doesn't work out you can let them go early and clearly according to your very clear upfront MSOP's, KPI's and JD's, as it will be obvious to all if these are getting met or not.

Don't try to cut corners on hiring the best, but here are some low cost, high life methods to create a high business life when starting out:

Hire your Mum's! Rob and I hired both our Mum's as out first 2 staff members, paying them virtually nothing yet they were both troopers for us. We didn't have money to burn back when we started so we leveraged the goodwill (and boredom/retirement) of our Mum's and they helped us grow the business on low cost. Mum's, we love you. Get friends and family to help where possible; you can always pay them more later or give them a share in your business.

a. Hire staff who can directly bring revenue to your business, especially as you start. If each of your first 5 staff members brings in around 2 times their salary in revenue, and sales bring in 3 to 5 times; you have the foundations of a great business. Don't hire deadwood and stay lean.

b. Hire per hour or per minute. In the new age of web and social, where all you need is a laptop and an internet connection to get started in business, people work online with virtually no overhead, and their lean nature means you can reduce much of your staffing costs. There are many outsourcing websites such as peopleperhour, elance, alldayPA, where you can hire people for one off jobs online, and PA services by the hour and sometimes by the minute. It means zero wastage, and a low cost start as you only pay for what you use, which might only be 10 hours when you start. Get into the habit of outsourcing as much of your admin as you can early, way before you think you need a full time PA, and you'll free up most of your working day for Income Generating Activities (IGA's).

c. Hire people in sales roles who are used to low basic, high commissions. People used to this remuneration set up know how to bring in revenue, and keep your overhead low. They'll often/mostly be very self motivated, and you can keep your cost base down. Estate Agents were a ripe source for us, having hired many of them over the years. Many end up earning between 2 and 4 times their basic with us in commissions, but if they don't bring in any sales or purchases, the risk is reduced and the costs are low.

d. Get recommendations for staff. Over the years we must have spent a six figure and more sum on recruitment fees. I've studied our best sources of talent (ads, recruitment agencies, referrals, social media) and there doesn't seem to be a direct correlation between source and talent.

One thing that hurts my aversion to spending is wasted recruitment fees. We have found some great talent at Progressive through asking on social media posts, and posting job ads in the Progressive communities and forums. We've also found some great talent through referrals, and we pay our staff a commission if they introduce someone who we hire. This is not a perfect art, and must never bypass your recruitment/ interviewing process, but can save good money that you can compound over the next 30 years or more for income.

e. Train your staff well. The highest cost in staffing is not actually recruitment fees, it is replacement costs. James Caan, a friend of ours who runs a recruitment company, believes it to be as high as £20,000 or more to replace a staff member in training time, lost revenue in the changeover and trainee period, advertising and occasional tribunals. We've lost staff in the past because we haven't trained them properly, and this was totally foolish as we were paying twice over for them in reality. take the time to train and mentor, and you'll have low cost recruitment and high life talent.

f. Get good HR advice. When you start and keep costs low, you won't hire an internal HR manager, but you can either read/study this as you get to around 5 staff members, or you can outsource to a consultancy who can advise you on best HR and employment law. The law is not as obvious as you might think, and many a business owner will tell you that it's weighted heavily in favour of the employee. Ignorance is NOT bliss in this instance, and you need to know the law. A good advisor can help you with hiring, performance management, grievance, holiday, sickness and dismissal where necessary. It's worth the low cost.

g. Remove deadwood. Letting people go isn't one of my favourite parts of business, but as you grow you accept that it is part of the journey. If you are soft, don't like conflict or just plain don't like the hard conversations, you'll open yourself up to having other staff members poisoned by people in your business who shouldn't and don't want to be there. I now have the opinion that if they are not happy or not performing in the role, it isn't right for them, and so I owe it to them to question this, and if agreed to be true, an agreed parting of ways that is as right for them as it is for us. Anyone left too long in the business that isn't right will cost you dearly.

## 2. Marketing

If any pound spent will give you the greatest value to your business in addition to good staff, it is a well spent £ in marketing. It hurt to see Bob do such great marketing for Acorn, and this was something that Rob immersed himself in with little budget, probably with an Axe to grind and a point to prove. If you spend money on targeted marketing where you can test and measure the results and returns on investment, then you will increase revenue and profit faster than we did when we set up Progressive. You can also test which areas of marketing spend work and don't work, and scale up and back accordingly. The only way you know is to test, but we were paranoid about spend so started too slow and small in hindsight.

This is an area that lends itself perfectly to the low cost, high life mantra. Here are some low cost ways to create your high life business:

a. Social media. I was slower than some on social media, as I wanted to see the proof that it wasn't just an excuse to do no work and moan about everyone in public. Social media platforms such as Facebook, LinkedIn, Twitter & Google+ have proven to be great for getting your message and brand out there and seen. You can reach millions of UK potential customers in minutes, and in the true low cost high life fashion; it's free! The only investment is your time in learning how to master the platforms and then becoming visible and active. If you type 'Progressive Property Community' into Facebook you'll find a private Progressive group. If you type in Progressive Property you'll find a public one, and if you search for my name we can be friends :-)

b. PPC (pay per click). PPC is a direct marketing method to pay for clicks and 'opt ins' to your business. You start up simple, fast ads on platforms like Facebook, Google & Bing, and in minutes you can have your ads seen by your exact, targeted customers. It was around a decade ago that this changed the face of advertising forever, and levelled the playing field for the small start up vs. the huge companies with TV advertising budgets. To keep PPC low cost, target only the specific groups of customers you know are buyers according to the exact keyword matches, and start with a small daily budget; say £10. Then test your adverts and 'landing pages,' so that you aren't wasting money, until they convert at a high percentage. The marketing department at Progressive are currently getting a new lead/customer at an average cost of not much more than £1.

c. JV's (Joint Ventures). If you have a product or service, and can find someone with an active customer list, you can cut a low cost hit results deal. Offer them a juicy commission or share that they can't refuse, and they will promote your offering to their bulk list of customers at no cost. If you have your own customer list it can be an even lower cost, because in return for your send to your partners database, you send their offer to your customer list with no payment changing hands.

d. Referrals & birddogs. Referrals speak for themselves. I love referrals as a marketing model because they cost you nothing, and they are the most willing customers to buy. Most businesses aren't active enough in referrals, and get them through chance or because they offer a good service, but don't create a strategic plan to grow their referral network. Because marketing can be very expensive and wasteful, you should invest time into your 'Birddog plan.' A Birddog is a gun dog that goes and brings your game back to you after the hunt, and thus an apt name for a targeted referral. Reward and show appreciation to your existing customers for referrals. Pay them fast. Hand cheques, take photos and share on social media. Ask them for more. Have a league table so that they can compete against each other. Have a sliding scale reward system if they pass a certain amount of business to you. Rob and I take our best 'Birddogs,' up in the Helicopter when they hit a certain number, and the feedback is that it is a nice touch. If you want to drill right down and gain great knowledge in this area, I recommend 'How to sell anything to anyone,' by Joe Girard, quite possibly the best book written on this subject. For less than a tenner your customers can grow your business for you; how's that for low cost, high life?

e. Email marketing. I'm continually amazed at how few business owners don't regularly contact their customer list. It's not a lot of effort to ensure every business card and contact is entered into an email service system like iContact or iSoft, and then contacted with value added information 1-3 times a week (depending on your industry or niche), and then a respectful offer every 4-5 emails. In the world of marketing online, the size of one's email database is likened to the size of a certain part of their anatomy, and the common saying is that the value of their business is in their 'list,' or database. This will only cost you on a size of consumption basis, so the costs will be very low until you have a large customer list.

f. Exhibitions. This is not the lowest cost marketing strategy on my list, and I wouldn't have added this a few years ago, but we've done thorough testing of this method and it has produced significant ROI for us. We didn't exhibit at shows/exhibitions when we were smaller, so I recommend 2 strategies. When you are small and lean and on a shoestring, go to the big 'expo's' in your niche as an attendee. Go around every stand, get to know the business owners, and perform some Guerrilla marketing (free marketing) strategies to meet customers. Who would know if you are exhibiting or not while you are there? In the early days Rob and I (when we were just Rob and I) met many customers and future partners at the Property Expo's. Later, once you have a marketing budget, exhibit to generate business. You must use the following strategy to maximum ROI and minimum cost. Wait until the last minute to book the stand, you will get 50% - 75% off the rate card price. Get the smallest stand that you can. Do not spend any money on the dressing of the stand; simply get some pop up stands/banners printed with your branding and offerings on, and pop them up. Then have a 'lead magnet,' which is something of high value that you will give away for free in exchange for contact details; say a book or valuable report or App, and then get as many contacts as possible throughout the 1-4 days of the show. Focus on this, not sitting in an empty stand wishing the time away or having long meetings. We once came away from a show with 800 contacts. That worked out at less than £3 per contact, and the LCV (Lifetime Client Value) of each average database member is between ten and thirty times that number.

g. Content marketing & blogging. Content is king, as they say. If you spam and sell sell sell then you may make some short term cash, but you won't likely build a large organic following and customer/brand loyalty. Make it your mission to publicise 1-3 great articles or value add pieces a week and post across all your marketing platforms. She who has the best content wins. Again, this is low cost and creates high goodwill. I recommend you follow Seth Godin to see how he does it. Also, there are many people in the new social world who've built 100,000's or 1,000,000's of followers on their Blog because of great content, and then gone on to sell the same number of books based on the goodwill of their valuable information. Search 'Progressive Property Blog,' if you'd like to receive our property information for free.

h. Video marketing. Video marketing is more powerful than other media because people can see and hear you, and get more of a connected sense of who you are, without risk. How do you feel when someone has a Facebook profile but no photo? If you're not producing video, people can't connect with and trust you at a deep level. If your videos are good then people will share and spread them for you, and they rank very well on search engines too. It's also easy and low cost, because you can create them on your smart phone, even edit them with free Apps, and then share them on free social platforms. Ohhhhhhh YES!

h. Webinars. Online training platforms and webinars allow you to give people prolonged trainings for free or at low cost so you can build trust and earn the right to sell your offerings. You can promote them through social networks and email marketing, and have 100's or 1000's of potential customers try you out at low risk. Rob once ran a webinar with just over 1,000 people on it and gave some valuable information and then offered membership to our online Property Portal. Off the back of that webinar we gained monthly membership revenue of over £30,000 per month. Low cost, high sales for you. I recommend Google Hangout or GotoWebinar (part of GotoMeeting)

### 3. A real office

In the early start up days, we set up Progressive in Rob's dining room that was too small to dine in, and it served the low cost purpose. As we got busier though, this became a false economy. Although you want to keep costs down, if you have an office in a shed for client facing businesses, as Progressive was, you won't drum much business because you won't look established enough. We lost clients because we brought them to a half empty office that looked like we'd just set it up for the meeting. Whether you use a shared facility, or some of the great and cost effective office and meeting room services that you get with serviced offices now, it is essential to have space that looks worked and lived in, and even the right address perception in some industries, so clients get a sense of longevity and trust, when starting up. As you grow your challenge will be keeping it clean!

I wouldn't change much else, and have no regrets to the tight-fisted nature that we run the ship. Our low cost base enabled us to have a delayed high life where so many others struggled. Sure, we probably missed a few boats, but we're still sailing and as most businesses don't make it through the first year, I'm certainly proud of what Progressive has achieved.

## Progressive Progression - Summary

Leverage & outsource before you need to. Whatever you can pay to save yourself time, do it, because focusing on small economies is the fastest way to get poor. Leverage projects not just tasks and give your team crystal clear instructions. Get constant feedback and get their 'buy-in' on projects & roles .Invest your time rather than spending it. Think 'who can I get to do it?' Build a team. Be aware of different aspects of your business. Manage strategically not emotionally. Lead, but let them crack on & don't micro-manage. The opportunity cost is huge. Leverage 1st so that you can free and buy back time then utilise that saved time to make money and do the things you love.

# 13. Off a cliff

By the end of 2007 our assets were helping us grow steadily and securely, the kind of growth I like. We had many contacts through networking events, our email database, we were using Google adwords (PPC) effectively to generate great marketing spend returns, we had our first book written, and our plans for growth for year 2 were aggressive. But during the summer I'd been watching the sub-prime crisis unfold in the US. American institutions were dropping like flies, and in Sep 2007, while on a trip to Florida in the Ritz Carlton on Miami Beach, I picked up a newspaper and saw queues of people outside a branch of Northern Rock. Until this point, I hadn't really taken the crisis seriously, but now it was real. Over the next year things got progressively worse in the financial sector and I was very concerned about what this might mean for our business.

But by now Progressive was doing well. We had good systems for lead generation and bespoke property management. We had started running our own events as I'd seen how effective they'd been for Chris and Marie at Acorn and the partner events we attended. We were building a strong following of people who wanted to learn how to do what we had done in property. We'd passed fifty property purchases and Progressive looked like it had solid foundations. However by the end of 2008 our model of building Handsfree portfolios for clients looked in jeopardy due to the drastic and unexpected economic changes. Remortgaging homes to get capital and getting mortgages to buy investments was much harder, and the news and reality of the recession and credit crunch was starting to hit home.

The events that we'd been running to present our Handsfree model had to quickly convert into events that would teach people how to invest themselves, with various courses and programs. This was a vital turning point in Progressive because companies in our industry were dropping like flies. We saw a 'contrarian,' opportunity for ourselves and investors to cash in on the panic and (learn how to) buy cheaper properties at bigger discounts with higher cashflows. The Handsfree model could still work, but not to the scale we had planned for. The future was uncertain and there were no guarantees on liquidity of lending, plus we felt people may tighten their belts, so we needed more accessible, lower price point offerings. This was a big 'low cost, high life,' opportunity, and the only way to keep your business sustainable and operational through these times.

We were right to move quickly because this was just the start; no one could have predicted the apocalyptic effect, and because property is so closely linked to the general economy, our industry was about to have an atomic bomb dropping on it. At the end of 2008 Lehman Bro's went bust and the recession in the UK was official. It was clear that this was not going to be a short downturn, and everyone was digging in for a long bleak period. The banks unwillingness to lend caused us to quickly revise our models and change the way we bought properties.

*(NOW) Even though we hadn't designed it, and we didn't think this at the time, the timing of the credit crunch and global crisis for Progressive was actually good. We had low overhead, we were lean and flexible and were not over exposed in properties and client deliverables. This meant that any downward movement in the market or recession of the economy wouldn't hurt us (fatally, at least). We were adaptable. We had very few staff. We could decide quickly and move fast. This was a big lesson, and as we grow, I still see vital importance in reacting to the market and moving fast. This becomes your competitive advantage when others are too slow, corporation-like or just can't adapt quickly enough. Never get too big or systematic to react quickly to change. As Warren Buffett says: 'Be fearful when others are*

*greedy, and greedy when others are fearful.'*

Our industry was decimating around us and competition much bigger than us went pop and bang on what seemed like a weekly basis. The biggest names in the industry, with one company valued at over £160million, went bust. The most common ones were the new build/off plan/overseas brigades, with finance for these properties the hardest to obtain due to the highest risk to the banks. We were determined not to be one of them and so tightly controlled costs and proceeded with operational caution but aggressive marketing to take an opportunistically larger market share. The £millions per month that the biggest property training provider was spending was now a gaping hole for us to attempt to fill, and with a model we felt was more sustainable and easier to obtain finance for. We had increased positioning and brand strength by default for still being there.

Chris had shown us what happens when you are frivolous, so we felt like we were armed with more knowledge than others around us, we'd had the 'how NOT to,' education and our determination not to end up like Acorn was the strongest motivation to succeed. Despite the pandemic fear, we knew from history that the best and biggest buying opportunity for 15-20 years was coming, and this was our big chance. Once the dust settled and we felt that the market had done most of its falling (this is difficult to predict as there is a lag in property behind the real economy and then the stock market), we started to scale up. Our clients and ourselves bought a stack of bargain property between 2009 and 2011 at firesale prices which I doubt I will see again. But I'll be ready if we do.

## Contrarian opportunity

Initially rents fell as the market turned down in 2008, but this soon reversed as less people could buy. The more the banks clammed up (by

2010), the more the government took it upon themselves to instigate stimulus. Interest rates plunged to 0.5% and they set the printer presses rolling to massively increase the money supply. Stories of impending hyper-inflation and rampant market rises all turned out to be hyperbole. Inflation stayed around or less than 3% owing to the massive deflationary pressure present in the economy. Real wages were on the way down as more people got laid off. Companies started discounting and banks held on to their capital reserves, as they could not access the wholesale markets for funding. If the markets weren't lending to the banks, the ones that relied heavily on this type of funding began to fail. Bradford & Bingley, Northern Rock, RBS, Halifax and later Lloyds effectively went bust, and the government had to step in to support them. Using taxpayers cash, they provided massive loans and/or injected capital in return for ownership. Some banks such as B&B's mortgage arm, Mortgage Express, reduced services down to a level where they don't do much more than collect mortgage repayments and recover loans. These are being wound down slowly by the government and many are still operating in this way today.

With Bank of England base rate at 0.5%, many of these loans were now either side of 2%. Such was the way these mortgages were designed; the banks had/have no choice but to continue charging a rate which tracked the BoE base rate of 0.5%. This has made these loans very cheap for many investors, and saved many of them from losing their properties, or worse, bankruptcy. But this has massively reduced the banks' revenue, meaning some lenders are looking at ways to recover these loans. I know one particular investor who has more than 150 of these loans with one lender, having borrowed about £15million, who is now paying 2.25% on most, or around £325,000 per year. This represents a saving over current rates of around 2% or £300,000 per annum. Existing properties on these terms became even better/bigger cashflowing properties, and despite the drop in value, keep bringing in the cash. We are fortunate in that we had dozens just like this too. Low cost, high income.

The banks also suffered a double whammy hit in that the FSA (now FCA)/BoE was demanding they hold more capital to protect them in the eventuality of a large number of their loans becoming 'impaired,' (late payments, arrears, bad debt). Capital hoarding became very much in vogue, and the banks clammed up even further lending even less to homeowners and investors. By the end of 2010 however, lower interest rates and money printing had still pushed up house prices by around 10% in the Midlands (they fell by around 30% in some areas in '07), and the stock market had seen an adrenaline boost.

*(NOW) Contrarianism*

*In 2006/7 prior to the struggles in the US, property was widely accepted to be a great investment. By the end of 2008 it was like you were wearing a pair of dirty Y-fronts on the outside of your trousers. If we mentioned to anyone in passing that we had a property business and portfolio, they would look at us like we needed to be taken to the hospital immediately and assume our world was doomed. Responses like 'it must be so hard I am so sorry for you,' were common. I gave up trying to explain to people that we were coming into a beautiful buying opportunity. The truth was that by the end of 2009 the bottom had just passed (so it seemed) and conditions were good enough to clean up. 'Whilst we still had to work for deals, implementing major leafleting campaigns and getting as many Estate Agency contacts on side as possible (it was not like the previous recession where interest rates went into double digits and more people got repossessed), there were plenty of deals to be had at great prices and high yields.*

*The masses believed that we should have stayed away from property because that was what the media was pumping out at the time. Our 'contrarianism detector,' told us to dig deeper, and being at the coal-face, seeing changes in the market months before they got reported to the Land registry or Halifax/Nationwide house price indices, the evidence and advantage was clear. Other famous investors and business people have already coined the phrase: 'observe the masses, do the opposite.' This mantra will serve you well in your investing career.*

*A note about the media. the media do not print normal, average, real life events. Life, day to day, is actually quite normal. Not many life changing, controversial or revelatory events happen over the period of 27,375 days a 75 year old lives. It might only be that something sensationally good or bad happens 30 - 100 times in those 27,375 days. But that does not make for good media. It does not sell papers. It does not create hype or frenzy. So the media exaggerate to the extremes, creating a sensationalist, abnormal view of reality to meet their primary needs; sell papers. No one would be interested in reading about the normal, boring 27, 275 days where not much happened. When things are good, people often think/assume things will stay that way (or behave like it will ad infinitum), and conversely when they are bad they behave like the world will end, not seeing that tomorrow could be very different. This is reflected in the media where news will always be over-hyped. It will be much worse (or occasionally much better) than the normal 27,375 day grind reality. House prices will only ever 'crash,' or 'boom,' and you'll rarely see any headlines that say 'Today house prices stayed the same.' This understanding of the way people and the media view events gives you a strategic, long term advantage.*

The Progressive Portfolio Builder model became easier once the market and confidence picked up, and more clients became interested again. Many people were 'fed up of being fed up,' and believed that the 'depression,' was coming to an end. We experienced the benefit of cheap house prices and high cashflow from low interest payments, and capital growth; a rare double benefit. People also wanted a better return than the paltry interest they were getting in the banks, confidence in banks, pensions and corporations was at an all time low, and many people wanted to/needed to take responsibility for their own pension, investments and future.

Rents started to rise significantly as the banks clammed up because less people were able to buy, so they were forced to rent. Yields (cashflow) therefore started to increase and all told (with the effect of the capital values being 20% less than '07) the peak yields were easily 2 percentage points higher than pre-crash years. This made incomes relative to capital outlay considerably better for investors. This 'rebalancing,' de-risked new investors' positions. By now we had traded over 350 properties and were managing over 200, which we either owned or had a Joint Venture in. The training arm of the business was showing fruits, and it felt like things were getting easier. Investments were now lower in cost and higher in income.

*(NOW) Reacting to the hand that the market deals you is a wiser strategy than bitching about it. As finance had become more difficult and people weren't just spending their remortgage monies frivolously, we found ways of creating and selling lower ticket items that didn't need such big and risky investment decisions. Courses, CD's, DVD's, books, online training; all still in demand and much easier to offer and lower risk than 'done for you,' services in the tens of thousands. This actually helped us gain a far wider market reach, even if the relative amounts were much lower. Now we had 1,000's of customers, not just 50 or 60, and so it created more brand awareness, reach and a broader referral network. And, unexpectedly, more Portfolio Builder clients.*

*In hindsight, starting with lower priced products and building up to larger services may have been the best way to go/grow, but we were well capitalised with higher fee products in the earlier days. It has become evident that there are strategies, products and services that work well in every part of a market cycle, and reacting to these cycles quickly and either evolving or revolutionising your products and services is essential for continued, long term business and portfolio growth.*

## Off a cliff - Summary

With change comes big opportunity and with fast change comes faster opportunity. It's survival of the fittest right now, and for those without the stomach for it, it's hard. But for those with courage who make decisions and take action, the money that the helpless masses are losing is up for grabs, and there's more of it than ever. Embrace the change and commit to being at the front of innovation. Look for the opportunities in change, and look to get in early [not first, but near the front]. Use the change to provide a service that most people need [in lieu of the change], and serve more people while they are struggling to adapt to the change.

## 14. No 'I' in team

By the end of 2008, we expanded to new offices and took our first (non family) member of staff on. This was an important moment as we'd broken the shackles of cost restrictions, and were finally in the mindset that to grow a substantial business, we needed to build a team. This was a mindset shift for me, as everything until now had been built on a low cost base. But I never wanted to be a one man band, so I know I had to embrace growth and take more (calculated) risks. I decided to dig around the Estate Agents I'd been using to source deals, unofficially interviewing them to be Progressive's 'Head of Acquisitions', on the ground, whilst viewing properties. We enticed two of the likely candidates into the office with the property ownership/investing dream that the best Agents have a hunger for, and employed them to take over the buying from me, so I could grow the business and spend my time on higher value projects.

We knew that these guys had all the experience in dealing with Estate Agents as they were Agents themselves. They intrinsically knew how the deal flow worked, how and where the best deals went, and how the system of who got the best deals worked. They also, valuably, knew all the other Estate Agents/Agencies on the local 'Estate Agents row.' Most importantly of all, they knew exactly what you had to do to get the best deals, before being listed in the window, and before other hungry investors got their mitts on them. And we'd seen the proof with our own eyes because they'd sourced deals for us; really great deals, and protected the sale. They had the contacts and experience and were solely focused on buying property. This freed me up to do other important roles in the business to keep it growing. Roles such as build the processes and systems of buying, building a team and the 'sales progression' process, keep my hand in getting new clients, and the financials and KPI's of the business. I was able to manage the business and work on developing it, rather than being in the thick of it. And I had an idea on how to grow the personnel on a low cost base.

*(NOW) To this day with the 100,000's of people we have trained through Progressive Education and our other companies, I see most of the Entrepreneurs acting as one-man bands; being the very obstacle to their own growth. They are always too stuck in the details of the business that other (maybe better, more experienced) people could do, rather than the strategic planning and management of their business. It is counter intuitive in that their beliefs of expensive payroll inhibits their growth and keeps them stuck doing those very things they don't like and keep them small. This was a hard habit for me to shake, but if I can do it, being 'Autistically averse,' to spending (as Rob puts it), then you can too.*

*What always comes to mind is a gun dog digging down a hole for a Rabbit, with your head down the hole and the mud flying between your legs, you get deep and deeper down, with no ability to look forward, back or up. How would you know if you're in the right hole if you can't see the other holes, the entire ground, and often digging so hard in excitement or ravenousness, that you can't even see forward. Most people are digging too hard to be effective or wealthy.*

*Rob and I are very different people with opposing skills yet a unified vision. We are both competent at the skills the other isn't weak at. My 'flow,' is doing deals, finance, running and implementing systems and developing investment strategies. However marketing, creativity, lead generation and vision are not strengths of mine but pure flow for Rob. Of course there is some cross-over, but our partnership has worked because there is enough that is different. We don't get in each others' way (too much). You get the freedom to focus on the things you are good at and enjoy, you don't step on each others' toes, and you get the leverage of further reach. You can't have a successful business that has great accounting systems but no marketing, and conversely a great sales focused business will fail if there is poor operations and delivery. In essence you get to do more of what you love and are good at by having a partner who gets to do what they love and are good at. This is liberating and stops a lot of the mistakes and stress business will inevitably bring.*

*Many business owners choose a business partner who is like them and has similar skills, like a pact you had at school with your best friend. This is a mistake in my view, and with the benefit of hindsight, not one I would choose. I have tried partnerships in the past with people who have a natural flow to do the same thing as me, and you end up following each other around sniffing each others' backsides, sometimes making the things you are good at worse because of the 'too many cooks,' syndrome. A much more powerful combination is when opposing skillsets dovetail, the sum of which is greater than the constituent parts. You get 'marriage value.' If two of you do the same thing, one isn't needed.*

## Young & hungry

Young, hungry 'Entrepreneurial,' type employees, such as ex Estate Agents, can bring great results for your business. But through experience, need careful management. When Progressive was small, we hired many self-starting 'Entrepreneurial,' type staff and they brought passion, energy, enthusiasm and hard graft to the party; essential when you are starting up. (Looking back, we hired a lot of people like us!). They are good at getting things done and developing new relationships, often with a bit of 'ducking and diving.' However as you grow, the ability to control them and keep them focused gets more challenging. They will frequently want to do what they want to do, can be belligerent, selfish, anti-authority and tough to manage. Just like I must have been!

The buyers and 'Entrepreneurial', staff we've had have been up to all sorts of mischief once they've gotten comfortable. Philandering relationships with our PA(s), virtually writing off one of my M3's, office flirting on a mass scale, setting up in business with our clients, fiddled expenses, snooping around on our servers, buying deals behind our backs; all just par for the course for an ex-Estate Agent. But this overt cheek makes them great at buying deals, so you take what hand you are dealt with, let them crack on with an occasional back-hand slap, and if you get two good years you've done well. They'll always chase the next biggest shiny object, or one day want to run their own business (started on the back of yours). Always a roller-coaster ride, difficult to control, but as long as you give them a good commission structure and give them enough freedom, they'll help you grow your business fast. Your culture will change and you'll hire other, more professional or corporate types when the needs must.

In the past we've even given shares to these types of employees, making them partners and shareholders, in an attempt to keep hold of great talent. Whilst I don't regret this, and would happily cut talent into my businesses, they rarely last, and you need to make sure you have a buy back clause.

## With growth comes change

As we've grown and matured, we've found it more important to have longevity, especially with staff, in our business. Recruitment fees and cost of getting staff trained and up to speed can cost £10,000's, so having an average lifetime staff member value of twelve to twenty four months is expensive, and not inline with the 'low cost, high life,' methodology. Whereas staff turnover is simply part and parcel of business, you want long staying steady staff to help you grow into the future. Not everyone is a shining star (that burns itself out quickly), and those who are more consistent, reliable, honest and likely to stay with you for the long haul offer great(er)value. We've been fortunate in attracting more people like this as we've developed a more professional structure and deeper org chart. Most have been found in an existing role, often in larger entities proving loyalty and longevity. As much as I hated the thought of paying recruitment fees, and becoming overly corporatised, our previous policy of 'selling the dream,' to unproven, energetic youth only lasts so long, and bridges you so far. I now have a policy that I will only hire someone if I am more than happy to pay 15% in recruitment fees (even if sourced without recruitment agents). The lower cost is in longevity, and the lower risk is seeing them in a role, exhibiting that in another company.

## Management

In investing and business, the single most important aspect is ongoing management. Your stock and property portfolio, your asset allocation, your business and staff all need ongoing management and maintenance to continue to pay you a dividend. Nothing stays the same, and if anything is left long enough, it will decay or die. I don't profess to be a Harvard management guru, but my on the ground management of various asset classes, people and businesses has taught me these main (low cost) lessons:

### 1. KPI's

What can't be measured can't be managed. It is important to have regular checks and meetings with staff or your portfolio. Key Performance

Indicators (KPI's) are simply measureable goals specified and detailed to measure the performance of an asset, individual to that given asset. This 'dashboard,' mechanism gives you instant insight into the performance and health over the previous timeframe, giving you the non-biased reality and early indications of change. The more you can see on your dashboard, the lower the 'irregular shock,' costs will be, and the higher the results. These can be for sales, operations, purchases, costs, rentals, business plan and even admin. You have a consolidated, proven, quick glance guide that helps you make fast, decisive and accurate strategic decisions that help your business or asset grow.

Call me a skeptic, but I've found that people lie to protect their best interests or ego, so the only real measure of the reality position is measurable data. And to keep damage costs down, a random spot check keeps people on their toes of high performance and systems running smoothly.

## 2. Management Accounts (Monthly)

Accurate management accounts are the absolute litmus test of the performance of the business or asset. Everything else is an opinion or guess. These give an historical view (lasts month, year on year) on the actions you took a quarter or half year previously, and are the most accurate platform to base future decisions. These will lag the KPI's, which can be kept up to date; often 3 days to a week accurate. It will take a little resource to get these up and running but will definitely save you money and keep costs down as you scrutinise the overhead. I must confess to enjoying this (perhaps a little too much). It took us 3 years to get proper and as close to real time management accounts for our business, which makes me conclude that all of our decisions in the first 3 years were instinct or guesswork. We must have done OK to that end, but I do not like making important decisions like that, even though staff and others will push you to make 'off the cuff' decisions. In retrospect, we should have created measureable KPI's and management accounts far sooner than we did. Simply looking at how much cash you have in the bank does not give you anywhere near an accurate position of the business. That would have increased costs and encouraged bad decisions, for sure.

## 3. Cash piling

The most effective way to ride any cycle is to sit on mountains of cash. Cash protects against most eventualities that pop up to bite you. You can not live a high life on low cash. I have seen so many businesses fail simply through burning all their cash: known as 'burn rate.' I've seen good models fail due to running out of cash. It is wise to have six months to a years existing running cost (burn rate) in cash holdings, at least if possible. Of course when you start you are more hand-to-mouth, so aspire to this as you grow and delay the gratification of unnecessary spending knowing that you will have a long future of spending in the mature years. Six months of running costs can turn into twelve to twenty four if you have to scale back through harder times, and is like a reserve of food to see you through a devastating natural disaster. I have also found that when you have these cash reserves you don't need them, and when you don't have them, you wish you did! A high life is created through living off income, knowing you have abundant cash protection, and next month that income comes in all over again. A low life will result in eating into cash reserves, leading to bad debt and emotional struggles.

## 4. Micro management?

People don't like being micro-managed. However, results are my concern, and of course in the long run they make the team member happy too, even if they needed a little push in the process. Staff will happily spend someone else's (your) money, so train your team members well but let them learn and grow and assist them to this end without standing over them. Give them specific and measurable KPI's for their specific role, and then let them crack on. In an idyllic world this would be enough for them to be top dog for many years to come, but the reality is that every now and again you will need to stick your beak in and make your presence felt. An intentional reminder and a little heat, though in the moment perhaps deemed as micro-management, will remind the team member that you are watching and results are expected. This will often be welcomed as there may have been some knowledge deficit, and if it causes tension, it simply proves the necessity. Over management will cost you your time when you are paying someone to do the role, but no checking will cost you in mistakes and unnecessary over spending.

## 5. Random spot-checking

It is important when managing that you know how to do the role you are managing, ideally having done it for a good period of time. This experience gives you the insight to check that the team member is executing properly. You can check viewings sheets, spreadsheets, mileage and time logs, meeting appearances and diary entries for correlation. You can then have a passing chat to customers, agents, solicitors, vendors and suppliers on the fly to corroborate what you're being told to ascertain feedback on your staff. Are they doing the job? Are they doing it well? These random and confidential off the record chats and checks give you the external truth of performance, and word will likely get back to the team member, letting them gently know that at any time you may (randomly) check performance. This will keep costs and costly mistakes to a minimum.

I like checking mechanisms to be 'physical.' The age of electronics has created great steps, but often everything in the 'cloud,' becomes invisible. I like to hold hard copy of everything important – I have a box file for each property with title deeds, mortgage documents and important information in. Of course you end up needing to buy your own storage facility to hold them all, but if I can see it, I can manage it and I don't forget it. This has helped immeasurably over the years in effective management.

## 6. Clarity

Clarity is one of those basic fundamentals people overlook because it is so simple. In a world of noise, clarity has become a complicated secret weapon, and I'm constantly amazed how people lack so much clarity in diction, vision, pitch and model. Less is more, and being crystal clear in communication, responsibility and most importantly expectation is vital. If it takes repetition and some patronising, so be it. When anything becomes confused, nothing happens, and most excuses are born out of a lack of clarity. Choose every word you say in business carefully. Set clear expectations, timeframes, instructions and deadlines. I know many billionaires who hate having their time wasted, and every word is money. Think and plan your pitches, presentations, meetings and speeches. Get feedback on your message, follow up with emails to double-clarify, never assume something is understood, make sure it is. Be clear on your investing rules, you vision and your goals. 'A confused mind says no, a clear mind says go.' Probably one of Rob's (cheesy) quotes! The high life comes from high clarity.

## 7. Consistency

Chris was a prime example of why and how inconsistent behaviour produces poor results. His mood swings, lack of clear direction and caffeine-rush based management created a lack of clarity, confidence and respect, and created resentment, tiredness of constant change for changes sake, and so less desire to work for him. Consistency takes measurement, note taking and organisation, strategic thinking, control of emotions and a removal of personal ego; not always easy to do, but worth the effort.

## 8. Relationship balance

There is a fine line between having a good relationship with team members, creating a shared excitement, ethos and vision, and creating too much familiarity. In the earlier days of Progressive we were very social with our team members; going out on weekends, going to the gym and such that this familiarity, although empowering in the early stages, breeds a flippant attitude to instruction and over familiarity. Not only do certain members start to take advantage, others in the team can become resentful. When you are more emotionally involved it makes it much harder to make the tough non performance driven decisions. Conversely, your team members need to know you care, feel loved, important and involved, and that you are an approachable person. If you are cold and corporate they'll have no desire to pull for you or feel part of something special and unique.

Some of the best feedback we've had for Progressive is that we are the best company to work for because people have autonomy, feel part of something that they can make a difference towards, and have genuine status and relevance. Give your team members this feeling without getting so close they lose respect for you.

# No 'I' in team - Summary

Hire a great team early. Hire a team before you're ready, because you'll never be ready. Pull in all resources you have, to get other people working for your vision. Take small, steady, calculated risks & keep a close eye on your team. You can always reverse your decision, but you can't buy the time back. When you get people working for your vision, they will feel part of it. And they can grow with it. Because your vision is aligned with their vision. Leverage behaviours & systems of the rich if you want to create a business independently of yourself, if you're ever to grow and be congruent with your chosen lifestyle.

# 15. Nearly 30 lessons by 30

By the time I'd hit the wrong side of 30, Rob and I had broken through 200 property investments and I'd had experience in investing in property, stocks, bonds, art, watches, wine (though non seriously), staff assets, cars (limiting depreciation) and building businesses. This represents my biggest life's passion, and along the way travelling up and down the coal-face I've learned many lessons, most of which through making small, low cost baby-step mistakes (and a few giant ones). Property has evolved to become my investment of choice and focus because it has given me the best returns and I've been able to learn leverage techniques that give it incomparable ROI figures. That is not to say that I have stopped all other investments, as that is not smart in creating a future-proofed investment portfolio. How to build wealth, how to grow wealth and how to keep wealth all require different strategies and asset classes, and your strategy will stay fluid as it grows. Here are the rules I've followed and now live by that when implemented can make you wealthy for the long term and give you the low cost high life:

## 1. Rules

Many people hate rules. I certainly like breaking harmless and irrelevant rules imposed upon me, and have a bit of 'I'll go and do the exact opposite of what you just said,' about me, much to Gemma's dismay (my partner). However when it comes to investing, rules are what create wealth. You simply must create/model rules that are proven to work, and then stay patient and disciplined to follow them for the long term, with faith along the way when you don't see instant results. The great benefit of rules is that it makes decisions relatively easy, emotionless (or at least emotion proof) and predictable. It also keeps costs to a minimum because mistakes cost money, and gives you the shortest route to the highest life. It sounds easy in practice, but the reality is that many people don't have the personality, belief or mentality to stick to rules. Creative types need to control their desire to do something new too frequently, and those who get bored easily should understand that if your systems and strategies get boring they're probably working! Simply stick to well tested rules and let compounding, leverage and long term-ism kick in and do all the work for you.

## 2. Discipline

All humans are ruled by emotion, except me (according to Rob). Success in investing is about tempering your 'instant quick fix,' emotion. If you eat too much food because your eyes get too big, you suffer the consequences. If you react angrily to a situation, you almost always wish you had reacted differently when you have calmed down. Investing is the same; it is about masterful control and awareness of your emotions, and kicking in logic at the point of weakness. One of the worst emotions that holds most people back from a high life of wealth is the 'retail therapy,' emotion. This must be controlled and mastered. I am not just talking to the ladies here, either. Attaching emotion to buying depreciating non-assets will ensure a high cost low life. I've never had this disease, but I had a somewhat eccentric upbringing. My business partner Rob loves to spend money on watches and cars and designer products; and impressively I have seen him go from a lot of debt that it got him in, to becoming very wealthy in a short space of time. He used one technique that mastered his spending of money, and I will share that with you later. I actually have the opposite emotion, I enjoy not spending money on non-assets. If you have retail-therapy-iris, perhaps you can attach the same emotion to saving or not spending the money in that moment in time, and imagine how much that saving will compound over 30 years and how much income that saving will give you passively from the asset it buys. Another emotion based money drain is holidays. For sure everyone needs to relax and recover in their marathon-not-sprint business life, but dropping £5,000 on credit (debt) to go a cheesy resort to run away from problems for a week, only to have the non-perfect holiday and then have to spend 3 years paying it off once you're back in the UK is financial suicide. Some short term delayed gratification is in order so that you don't have the long term regret. I will give you some strategies to get the lowest cost, huge benefit holidays later in the book.

Control the emotion of following the herd and believing the mass media. Your emotion will want to run with the tidal wave, but it is nearly always the worst thing to do. Let your logic kick in, reflect on history and what you know to be fact, and focus on that. Control the emotion of what non-specialists and novices impose upon you. Others' opinions when imposed with conviction can falsely influence your thinking, because in life those who shout the loudest usually win the argument. Remember they are not you, they don't have your knowledge, experience or motives, and they are reacting in an out of control manner to their own emotions. Control the emotion of how the naysayers affect you. They don't have your aligned values or motives, often reacting to an inadequacy in themselves. Stay away from forums or pity party unions. Control the emotion of fear. Control the emotion of doubt of your convictions. Control your emotions of (over caffeinated) excitement.

A way to do this is to take time out in your day to simply think. Evaluate in isolation your options, away from the influence of media and ulterior motives. The right answer usually comes to you. Of course when you are new or moving to the next level, you may not know the right, clear and obvious answers. It is vital to have mentors who are experts in different specialist areas; business, finance, life management, HR, property, fitness and so on. Surround yourself with those who are at a higher level than you in their specialist field, and the emotions will be more easily managed and the decisions clear from those who've trodden the path and made the mistakes before. Hiring a mentor is most often the lowest cost to reach the highest results. Some of my mentors are billionaires and talking about multi-million deals or business is simple and obvious to them. Many are also in their 50's and 60's; so a good 30 years more on the ground life experience to share with me over a 2 star Michelin dinner; which seems to encourage them to be open :-)

### 3. Supply & demand

Supply and demand curves are a fundamental concept when looking at any investment. To me they are like pornography. When you have limited supply of an asset and plenty of demand the 'give' that levels out the demand is the price rising. This keeps on happening until equilibrium is met where supply equals demand. The reverse happens where demand is low or there is plenty of supply, in this case prices will fall until equilibrium is met. I love UK property because I know both sides of this equation give good investment opportunities. Also, though we always seem to be striving for equilibrium, it never materialises because of human emotions. The imbalance (over and under) create investment benefits, and the cycle continually spins around too much or too little. There is a finite supply of housing in this country as the land supply is tightly controlled by our planning laws. Not being able to build in the green belt, developers are limited in areas in which they can buy and develop sites. As there isn't enough land supply, less properties get built than are required for the ever growing population, and prices rise over the long term. The demand side is also well dealt with as this is always rising in the UK. Population growth has been positive for many decades and continues to be so due to increased divorce, increased birth rates and increased immigration. The office for national statistics expects our population to be over 71M by 2030, an increase of around 10M people. Despite what successive governments have promised to do to reduce immigration, it continues and many new immigrants then have children which increases the population and demand for housing even further - a perfect recipe for a property investor. The same can not be said in the US where there is plenty of land to build new homes. Consequently it is pretty obvious that prices are unlikely (and haven't) to rise as much as the UK over the decades.

## 4. Price Limiting

When buying an asset, set your maximum 'walk-away', price based on proper diligence of the numbers. If the numbers don't work and you can't get your desired price for the asset, then change your investment strategy, walk away and DO NOT increase your price. The investment of time will create a sense that you'll have to do the deal to get that time back: this is an emotional illusion. Do not go into deals chasing assets you really want; you'll break your rules in an attempt to win. Do not go into deals trying to recover previous losses, you'll break your rules in an attempt to recover them. Do not go into deals because you are frustrated at a lack of progress, you'll chase shiny objects or over expose yourself. Remember you are in business and investing for the rest of your life; you don't have to do a deal everyday. You don't have to feel like you 'won,' or 'lost,' a deal, or to another investor. You just stick to your life long vision, knowing that opportunities present themselves daily and that some are right for you, and some are not.

## 5. Inactivity (Illusion)

Periods of inaction (a period of 'perceived,' non events) are also emotional illusions. Things do not happen in a linear fashion, they happen in waves, fits and starts. Waiting is as powerful as acting, if it is the right time to wait. If the deal doesn't fit, it doesn't fit. DO NOT try to make it fit; simply know that by waiting, you are in effect actively NOT LOSING. Not losing when the allure is present is as victorious an event as winning big and buying on value. Waiting through the previous recession and not losing money was in fact a victory. At this point the roots are probably growing, but of course you can't see them underground.

Sitting on your hands while others are making bad investment decisions is as smart a strategy as actively buying. Investing is as much about what you turn away as it is what you buy.

When you start out and don't have a refined buying strategy and it seems that others around you are buying in volumes, the temptation to chase burns and nags and eats inside. This emotion creates bad decisions, and because you have capital or time invested not earning money, you go and spend it, paying too much for the asset, buying completely the wrong one, or you take too much risk. You end up being busy for the sake of how it feels (and losing money on your time), or worse you make permanent losses. I have many personal examples of this, where a deal has taken so long that I've chased distracting ones. In 2008 I bought a 3 story house for £100,000 that quickly became worth 20% less because of the way the market was plummeting. I should have sat on my hands. Many of the older school investors effectively went on a years' holiday, as it was clear to them through experience where the market was going, but I didn't understand the lag and regretted buying this. I could recount many other stories that I regard as 'entrance fees.' I was itching to get deals done as I knew my time had come. I knew the market was becoming ripe from all the books I had read and people who I respected telling me that that was the case. Property is unlike the stock market which reacts very quickly tin comparison. It often lags by a year or 2 as prices adjust (because of factors such as liquidity). For the crash to fully play out you needed to wait from the end of '07 until March '09. With the help of hindsight I should have sat on my hands until this point. Easy to say now, but I will carry this experience through until the next part of the cycle. You can become a busy fool trying to push water up a hill. The crash was happening, I should I have just let it take place and waited until it had fully played out until I pounced.

## 6. Knowledge

This is frequently referred to in this book for a reason. Investing is about knowing more than almost all other people about a specific market niche, whilst having an eye on the macro (wider) picture. There are a finite yet large number of unknowns in any investment class which need to be removed through knowledge, experience and mentors. The fast removal of unknowns gets you closer and faster to the high life money. Knowledge reduces risk. The more specific knowledge you have, the fewer variables there are that are out of your control.

For example, when developing or refurbishing a property, the higher the level of your knowledge, the lower the cost will be; it is a direct correlation. The higher the valuation and/or sale price will be. The less unexpected costs and surprises there will be. The more confidence to proceed there will be. The higher competitive advantage there will be. As new opportunities arrive and the market moves, you will be much better placed to create opportunity or fix the issues that arise quickly and at low cost.

I have many examples of this. The first step is to healthily mistrust the quotes, specs and imposed knowledge of others who are 'pretenders.' Everyone has an opinion, and with (social) media it is easy to get your message out there and influence others. I have a simple rule with this: if they know what I need to know or have what I want: I listen. If they don't I (politely) don't. This rule has served me well, saved me 100's hours of time and made it easier to manage my emotions of doubt, confusion and overwhelm. The second step is to talk to and listen to those people who are doing what you want to do or are doing. The tips unwittingly flow out of their mouth. To them, their knowledge and experience is normal and easy. Suck these tips from them as if you can see the pound signs rolling out of their mouth and into your bank account. Frequently in developments I am involved in, costs and quotes are large. In a deal I have just exchanged on today as I (Rob) writes, the first quote to split electricity, gas and water for 29 flats was £150,000. To those in the know, this is an outrageous sum of money for the job, but on a build of multiple £millions perhaps others wouldn't know any different. However when dealing with monopolised utility operators, the perception or common knowledge is that you have no choice but to choose their 'service.' With the right knowledge I learned better ways to deal with utility companies and negotiate their costs. We managed to reduce the costs of an electricity service split by over £100,000 (on a quote of £150,000), this is a staggering saving. Lower cost for a higher life. £100,000 compounded over 30 years and invested in assets to produce income could replace a wage, on ONE deal/quote!

These 'monopolies,' prey on a lack of knowledge to profit. You counter this with a higher level of knowledge and therefore you're never the person who overpays because you don't know any better and you don't accept these quotes as the norm. This is another big reason to stay in your niche/industry for the rest of your life. Every time you start a new career/industry, you reset back to zero experience and knowledge. You have to make all the mistakes again, take all the risks again, and pay all the 'entrance fees', again. You don't have to be the quickest or the smartest, just be in it the longest; that is your most strategic advantage. Warren Buffett had read every book in his state Library on business and investing by the age of 12, and he is still in business and investing in his 80's, and I regard him as the prefect mentor.

A high level of knowledge attracts partners to you in a magnetic way. People actively hunt out those with expert knowledge in every walk of life, and you become an attractor of the best people because you are respected with the knowledge in your field. Water finds its own level, and the level of contacts I have met through the higher level network of people like James Caan, Neville Wright (Kiddicare), Sir Bob Geldof, Alan Sugar and many other non celebrities (many 1/2 or full billionaires) is unparalleled and instantaneous. This is far more powerful than being a good sales person, having the 'gift of the gab,' or networking like crazy. You will find your level of experts in other industries relative to the level of expertise you demonstrate in yours, thus it should be a lifelong commitment to keep increasing knowledge to keep growing your network. It costs nothing to attract these high life partners; they will find you organically because your name comes up in all the right conversations.

## 7. Cost balancing

Much of my childhood was about being schooled in cost saving attitudes and behaviours. Whilst beneficial when investing, saving and running businesses, it is only one part of the full picture. I will be brutal about the price of asset (or depreciating asset), but the big change in my attitude as I matured in business and investing is understanding what costs were necessary and seen as an investment. Sometimes, low cost means low/no profit. Know what to squeeze and what to grease. If you squeeze for a few hundred quid on important legal or conveyancing work, you'll get little to no service. You could even create resentment and intentional obstruction, and this tiny saving could be inhibiting the progress of a £multi-million deal. Often perceived 'expenses,' are actually an investment and an opportunity to grease some wheels to get deals though faster and cheaper to save much bigger chunks down the line. Your intuitive understanding of the difference will create compounded leverage and over time you'll spend frugally and invest wisely. Use your logic and experience to know the difference.

**8. Income supporting**

Any investment you are holding needs to be supported by income that it derives. Prior to the credit crunch, there were many investments available which were based on the value of the asset (such as property) increasing, rather than the actual income the asset would make every year. There are lots of investors in London buying properties based on the expectation that they will continue to go up in value which attract very low yields (income relative to value). Capital growth, though historical, is very unpredictable, where as income levels are more stable and guaranteed. If I can buy a property which will generate me a net 7% income (in Peterborough), why would I want to buy a property in London that yields 2%, just because I 'think,' that it may go up 5% more than the property in Peterborough in the next year. The same is true within any asset class being used for investment purposes. Why was I buying Jellyworks at 5p in the morning on the expectation that they would be a pound by the early evening, when there was equal chance that they could be worth zero? It's more effective to buy Philip Morris International and take their 5% plus dividend (yield/income) which has a much greater chance of being a reality. People don't look at the income and capital when making an investment, but you should. You can afford a much lower capital gain, if you have an income stream from the asset. IN fact, you'd be protected from a zero or negative capital gain if you have an income stream: you'll always be in profit and you'll easily cover the debt so the banks/lenders should stay happy. This exact thing happened to those who survived (and thrived) in the most recent property crash. Those who bought with income as the main priority survived, because as the capital values dropped like a bomb overnight, they still had the income to cover the debt and were still making profit. Those who only had a capital strategy ended up in 30% negative equity and were handing the keys back left right and centre.

## 9. Capital preservation

Capital preservation is also totally key to the investment story. You should only be investing in assets that are likely to preserve your capital, not erode it. Assets which experience wild increases in value are also likely to be putting your capital at an equally high downside risk. Capital preservation has to be consideration no.1 when deciding upon an investment because it takes so long to build it back up once it has been eroded. One years income often only builds 5% growth on the capital, so if capital is not preserved, it can take 15 to 20 years (based on having the same start up again capital) to build it back up, putting you decades back on your progress. Preserve capital at all costs. Have deep layers of capital reserves, and invest in assets that protect your cash from erosion and inflation. DO NOT put capital into non-assets/depreciating liabilities.

## 10. Long term-ism & delayed gratification

Investment returns are most powerful when they are compounded over time. Compounding is without doubt the 8th wonder of the world. You effectively get returns on returns, or interest on interest. £1,000 invested for 20 years on a 10% return (£100 income in year 1) will have grown to £6,727 in year 20, with no extra capital injected. The effect of compounded returns means that by year 19, the income has increased to over £611 per annum on original the £1,000 capital invested. This means that spending lots of money early on in your investing career will result in a huge loss of income/capital increase later, and it gets bigger the longer it is allowed to do its magic. I will show some specific, real life examples of the power of this in a later section.

Most people get excited by spending, I get excited by investing and delaying returns because of these key concepts. If you leave investments to compound over time, you can actually live off the interest/ compounded return, having all the things you want from the interest not the capital, preserving your capital and leveraging it to its maximum potential. Ohhhhhh YES!

In order to make real, sustainable money in this world, you have to do things others can't or won't. Very occasionally, there are ways to make quick money, but lasting wealth that creates a high life is usually only found through being in an industry or having expert knowledge over the long term. Like they say, it takes years to be an overnight success. The reason opportunities to make quick money are so rare is because anyone who spots them will quickly exploit them, closing the 'worm-hole,' opportunity. Those who make the apparent 'quick money,' have almost in every case had years of compounded experience to get them to that point of apparent 'overnight success.' The reality is that most people don't want to delay gratification or be in industries for the long term because it seems too difficult or sounds too much like hard work, and most people simply can't be bothered. I find this sad, and my aim in this book it to help overcome this short term, quick-fix thinking which actually most often leads to perennial unhappiness, or a high cost low life. Many search for the unattainable 'get rich quick.' If being a success in investing requires you to know at least as much, or more, and be at least as good, or better, than other high level participants, then being in it for a long period of time is your (only/best) strategic advantage. Things that glitter actually take you further away from this route. It is actually those who are in industries long enough to earn the right and be ready who get those quick/big win opportunities, NOT those who constantly search for them.

## 11. Mentors

Mentors are the shortest route to gaining better than the rest knowledge, because they short-cut all the mistakes and can guide you down the path of least resistance using their best experience and judgment. Mentors and power teams are the real, non get rich quick, get rich quick. I've had many mentors over the years, both official (highly paid) and unofficial (ethically bribed with help, ego massages, Helicopter flights and 2 star Michelin dinners). I usually decide that the best ones are those who are older, furthest down the road, doing exactly what I want to do and are where I want to be, and see me as no threat to them (i.e. not too competitive). Frequently those operating in a similar geographic area or of a similar age may feel threatened. A father/son relationship is particularly effective, where the older mentor can feel like he is disseminating value and passing on wisdom to someone who will actually listen, act upon it and get results. You'd be surprised how many older guys in property want a relationship like this because it can be a lonely business, their children didn't follow suit, or it aids their legacy. If you are of the age where it needs to be father/grandfather, so be it, and if you are of the age where you are the grandfather then I'm sure your peers will be too wise to feel threatened :-)

Paid mentors are (more) committed and have a genuine responsibility to help you because they are remunerated. They are forced into a service mentality, and know that there are repercussions of their advice, and so will take it more seriously. They will be better at holding you accountable to your success than the 'free,' or friendship types, and will often create/assist with goals and results over a specific timeframe, working with you between meetings and keeping you on track, supported and importantly, accountable. It also creates a traction and elasticity in you that compels you to act and get results, because you put (an often high) value on the mentorship relative to what you've paid. The fear of loss (of money and time) with paid for mentors is often the strategic advantage that makes you act on the advice and often, 'free advice is worth every penny.' Paying for mentorship cuts the noise and distraction away. It is, however, important to ascertain that the mentor you are 'employing,' has actually done the thing they are coaching you on. We run a years long mentorship at Progressive for would-be and existing property investors. Although more of an investment of funds and time than our courses, the best and highest level results come out of this because of all the factors in this paragraph. It is a (relatively) low cost for a high life.

'Free,' mentors aren't actually free and will need lunching, wining, dining and schmoozing. They might not command a direct fee, but it is important to give as much as you get and not just suck their blood, or the value of the relationship will fizzle out. You need to find out specifically what your (desired) mentor finds valuable: it could be recognition, playing a sport together they enjoy, fancy dinners and expensive wines, contra services or sometimes they may have their own children (around your age or father/son), and you can offer the interim-stage route for their children to learn from you. It can be a way for them to subtly place their children in a rewarding network.

The value from mentors is not simply knowledge. Your flow will determine which route works best for you, but I particularly enjoy socialising with people several levels up from me because I get to see how they deal with everything, not just property. It is these 'hidden gems,' that offer much of the best value; the things they do when they don't know they're being watched, their habits, behaviours and reactions, how they spend their money, where they spend their time and how they treat others. If, like me, you are fortunate to want to spend time dining and socialising with mentors in your personal and social time as well as your business hours, then this will come easy to you, and your results should too. Not forgetting, it is inspiring and motivating to sit opposite someone who is in the place you'd love to be in the future, and makes it ever closer to reality.

## 12. Risk

Risk is present in everything we do. In my opinion most people miscalculate many risks when investing. For example, many people would assume that the mere act of investing in property is 'risky,' made even 'riskier,' by a mortgage, where interest rates could double quickly. My father was too much this way in my opinion, and I had to break some of those shackles. Risk is about calculating what you can control, and what you can accept that you can't control. For example, interest rates can't be controlled, but the risk to you of their implications can be offset by / reduced by fixed rate or swap products or self insurance. I also hear people saying that investing in property is risky because the tenants might trash the house, not pay the rent, the rent may fall or other negative scenarios. With a portfolio of properties, the risk of a single tenant not paying the rent or trashing the place is supported by the others in the portfolio. Voids, bad debt, maintenance, even bad tenants are factored in to the income/expenses or insured against, giving the entire investment a controlled level of risk. The biggest risk is most often not taking charge of your financial future, investments or pension, or not taking action at all. This 'opportunity cost', is the biggest danger of all because it can't be measured but can easily be justified. It's not what it costs, it's the cost of not doing it that is often most expensive.

Property development poses much greater risks, as we saw in the late 80's and the recent recession of the late noughties. But this in turn can create higher rewards. The concept of building or converting a property usually requires a purchaser at the other end to buy a property from you. These purchasers can easily dry up and transaction volumes can plummet during times of economic crises. History has shown us that people have nearly always needed to rent, and I would recommend that any developer has the ability to rent the properties they are developing for the short-medium term should the market turn sour, keeping the income flowing to service the debt and keep the banks happy, protecting you from over exposure.

With risk, there is always a balancing act. What is too safe? What is too risky? People often believe, myself included years back, that the best home for their money is in an occupational or managed pension fund. Having walked like zombies into these vehicles, many people have experienced pitiful returns (sub 3%), 3 to 5 times lower than the overall blended return you might expect from a solid buy to let investment. Other stock market funds have their place for people looking to invest in a passive way, and whilst I hold stock (partly due to ISA tax advantages & as a hedge against the property market), they have a very high likelihood of producing a much lower return than a directly owned investment property (well sourced and managed). So what is the higher risk here? Going for the 'less risky', or taking a 'risk?' Is it best to risk nothing or everything? What is the risk of not investing? And what is your alternative?

The reality is that a return lower than the rate of inflation is a major long term threat to your capital. Earlier on, I spoke about 'capital preservation', being a major consideration when making an investment decision; here is your pointer: investments that are likely to return sub 3% don't just have a very high direct risk but have a guarantee of reducing your capital in real terms. Savings accounts with major banks/building societies are a great example of this, frequently offering interest rates of sub 1.5%. The bank is effectively saying to you that they will charge you 1% or more over the year for the privilege of lending your money out to others (probably for a property purchase!).

Whilst holding some capital in a bank account is essential for any investment strategy and balanced portfolio for cash preservation, or simply to conduct business due to its very high liquidity, I would suggest you keep this to a minimum. Granted, you may need to access cash quickly, but there are other liquid investments which will offer you much higher returns, beat inflation, and probably have a lower risk to your capital. This is especially pertinent as we saw the first round of 2 European banks (this time in Cyprus) using savers/depositors funds to effectively bail the bank out. Some savers lost up to 60% of their capital (over Euro100K) in one stroke. When the powers that be in the EU decided that this previously un-crossable line could be run over with a coach and horses, they changed many more seasoned investors/ business owners perception of the risk level of using a bank to deposit funds. High risk yet low return; go figure? Whilst the prospect of a UK bank or building society going down the same road seems less likely, the EU have made moves to make this style of non taxpayer funded rescue easier to repeat. Why the hell would you accept 1.5% (effectively eroding your capital at more than 1% a year plus after inflation) and have even the remotest risk that some management team within a badly run bank can use your cash to fix their mistakes (all sanctioned by the government)?

And people talk to me about property being high risk? If property is the alternative, I'll take it all day long.

One of the biggest risks to your wealth is inflation (increased cost of living) and the effect it has on reducing your *real* wealth over the long term. The interesting thing however is that when you borrow money exactly the same thing happens to your debt; it erodes. Even if you are just paying interest only rather than capital repayment, inflation is paying your debt down, let me explain this sex-like phenomenon:

Every year goods and services are likely to increase in price, in fact since I got into property properly in 2005 inflation has averaged over 3% annually or over 21% up to 2012 (source: BofE inflation calculator). Many argue that goods and services have in fact increased more over this period: think Petrol, foodstuff, cigarettes, flights/travel etc. I'm not here to argue the reality of actual inflation other than to point out that it is significant (especially when compounded). Companies have to pay their staff more wages to compensate for the increased cost of living, which shouldn't usually be an issue as they are taking more in sales due to inflation which increases their prices. This effectively means that a £100,000 mortgage taken out on interest only in 2005 is now worth around £79,000 in real terms (after taking inflation into account), which is a seriously powerful capital repayment 'system.' The increased cost of living is paying off your debt my friend! This is why I love (good) debt. If this was your cash it would have the opposite (negative) effect. The power of this over time is such that over a 25 year mortgage (taken out in 1987) with average inflation at 3.5% per annum or 87.5% in total by 2012 (Source BofE inflation Calculator). Effectively £87,500 of a £100,000 mortgage would have been paid off in real terms. This might be 1-3 months salary cheque to pay off the entire loaned capital on the property! Some may ask about the interest along the way, well this is covered by rent from the tenant in the property. The reality is that mortgage interest rates are currently barely more than the rate of inflation (and sometimes not even that). Even over the long term they have often not been more than 50% of the yearly rate of inflation, making debt a great deal if used properly and carefully on the right assets.

I have constructed a graph to show the effect of inflation from 2005 to 2012 on a £100,000 mortgage.

## Real Value of Debt (after inflation)

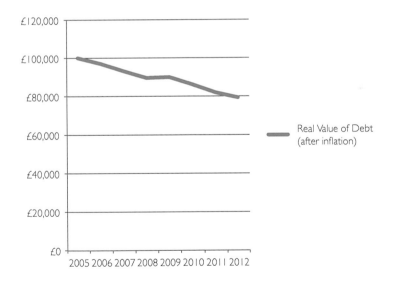

Who is paying for this? The savers who put their money in the banks who then lend it to you. These savers often end up with below inflation returns and you win by leveraging inflation in a positive, augmented way.

This invisible financial force can become your friend or foe dependent on how you use it. This should serve as a reminder as to why keeping large a percentage of your assets in the bank is not a good idea notwithstanding the issues I have spoken about above around the security of your money (post Cyprus).

So back to risk, there is a risk 'sweet spot,' individual to us all and market forces dependent. Your personal 'sweet spot,' of risk is in an investment you know really well and have done many times over, because knowledge is the best mechanism to reduce risk. What YOU control is less risky, because you know what others don't and you've battened down all the risk zones. You can implement strategies and stop losses to plug potential capital risks, and law or regulation changes have the least likely chance of 'pinching your principle,' because your knowledge creates solutions.

## 13. Investing Voyeurism

If I see a new investment or strategy, I like to stay on the periphery of it, maintaining interest, watching others do it and staying close to them, so I can understand the rules before committing any capital. I have no problem paying an 'entrance fee,' or a small beer as they say here in Barbados, but I don't want to commit significant capital on anything unproven. I want to see a full cycle of the investment with management accounts or proven returns. Sometimes the temptation is to jump in feet first to get early mover advantage, but this is high risk. It is often best to watch someone else doing it and learn vicariously through their experience, therefore controlling (your) losses, and getting the lowest cost education.

Once you have seen (what you see as) enough proof to make a start, dig deeper and get real financial proof and accounts, not just people's cries of instant success. People will nearly always declare positive results and huge returns because they are excited about their investment success, they want to vindicate their (often risky) decision and feel good about themselves. They have ulterior motives not to give you the whole truth, or to declare profits they 'will,' get (i.e. haven't yet) and therefore you can't base a serious investment decision on this. They won't know the reality for at least 6 months, and depending on the investment type (new build, off plan or overseas properties being a prime example) it could be 1 to 3 years or more. It's important to understand the detail and corroborate their responses with your own research. If you have any suspicion that they are misguided, simply move on and let them be.

In the past I have called people on their lack of fair analysis and been branded the naysayer. It's simply not worth your time and energy, and there's often no reason or benefit in doing this. If they are a friend, closer to you, you may want to help them. The best way to do this is simply to uncover the facts of the 'investment,' (I'm known for slapping together a nice spreadsheet) not commenting on whether good or bad, and they will make their own conclusion in the end and the friendship will be maintained. In the mid 2000's and through the crash I saw scores of investors and companies go 'pop,' overnight. Like popcorn they kept on popping. I know many of them or knew people who knew them, and so I studied it closely and voyeuristically, getting protected education as I could unravel how and why, yet not experience it personally and expensively. I wasn't there to judge or to condemn but to learn at lowest cost. Become a vicarious voyeur in investing for the lowest cost, highest return.

## 14. Mistake perception

Some people delude themselves that something is working to save face (or hard work), or because they don't want to feel (especially publicly) that they made a mistake. A mature investor will quickly accept his mistake(s), and often see it as a relevant lesson in the pursuit of success. This process of honesty (to yourself and others around you) is an essential trait of a wise, profitable investor. How quickly you recover from your mistakes and stop the losses measures your success and bank balance as much as your victories. If you kid yourself, it will cost you in the long run, people will trust you less and you'll have no 'room,' for investments that really work. Once you're sure an investment is a lemon, cut your losses quickly and move on, taking the important lessons and the opportunity to make a more sound investment replacement. Although at the time painful, people will respect you for this honesty and are more likely to warm to or partner with you. These investors/partners on the sidelines will be watching you on your investment journey, silently judging your actions remotely and seeing how you react to them.

You'll be surprised how your mistakes (and how you deal with them) attract partners as much as your victories. Many investors are afraid or closed with their knowledge, but as long as an investor isn't local to you and buying exactly the same property/investment types, this caution is usually misplaced; very much an old school psychology of lack/not enough to go around. People often don't appreciate that being open with critical and valuable investment knowledge specific to your niche pays huge dividends, because people will want to reciprocate. You'll end up with a much larger collective knowledge base and value any information given in a very high regard. I find it useful to watch what people do, not listen to what they say they are doing, as you get the greatest insight into the reality of what is working (and what is not).

## 15. The love of commerce

I'm a great believer in people doing what they enjoy and being in their flow. If you do daily what you wouldn't deem as work, then you are in 'flow.' If you can lose days at a time without looking at your watch, you are in flow. If other people are enthused just being around you and want to get into your niche from the passion you emanate, you are in flow.

If I have a spare moment, the things I want to do in my free time is look at the business section of the BBC news website, FT online, the economist, share prices and house price data. I'm genuinely interested in all things commercial. If there is any commentary on house prices, mortgage lending, economic changes and business news, I will dissect the article and search for the meaning it has relevant to my world of business and investing. No one has asked me to do this, no book has recommended the reading, it is not part of any course, it is not homework set for someone else, it doesn't have to be done for work, it is simply my free time hobby. I do get a little chastisement from Rob and the guys in the office for my somewhat analytical nature, but I hate watching sport, hate going shopping, can't stand soaps on TV, but love all things commercial, business and investing. This 'natural,' interest gives me an advantage in that I've already read up on and understand important details towards my investments before others are 'getting into work,' and 'working,' on it.

I can usually tell how successful an investor will be based on their natural interest in the area. If they're not entirely interested and have a 'natural,' leaning to other subject matter, they should leave investment decisions to other people. If you're not entirely sure if this area is your true passion, then spend time in your personal time reading and immersing in the subject. Notice if you find it fun or if you're always clock watching. Could you do this for the rest of your life, or could you find a way of making this enjoyable? There is usually a way if you are smart. To be honest, writing a book doesn't come easy to me, but with Rob typing whilst I'm looking out on the horizon at Sandy Lane, (and he's looking at the screen) we've managed to make it fun. Either get smart making business and investing fun and not like work, or do something else and give this book to someone who'd read it on the beach.

## 16. Buy (everything) low

One of the biggest fundamentals of investing is getting an asset cheaply relative to its 'market value,' or in the case of shares relative to your estimated value of the company and the estimated value it is likely to be worth in the future. This strategy de-risks the investment should the market fall, or you encounter other problems with the investment. Not only is your 'discount,' profit, it is a quicker exit and lower risk.

A 'discount,' gives you the greatest chance of obtaining a higher yield (higher income relative to the cost of the asset). Buying low gives you the biggest benefit of a higher likelihood of increased capital appreciation in the medium to long term, should you choose to sell or refinance. You will find it easier to obtain finance (banks, JV partners, bridging) if you have bought an asset low or under value, and you can often refinance out most or all of your capital from a deal, particularly relevant in property investing, or any asset you can leverage against. You will attract more private investors and JV partners, de-risking the deal and increasing their chances of profit (equity).

You need to drum this into your brain as a way of life. I find with most real investors I know that this becomes a compulsion and you'll even find them negotiating over the smallest things such as a taxi fare. In isolation it is easy to dismiss the power of buying something 5% to 25% lower than market value, but over time and across many purchases the compounded power is huge. It has caused me to develop an almost allergic reaction to paying full price for most things investment or liability based, and from a young age had a severe aversion to 'full retail price'. I get a great feeling when I get a 'deal', on something; on anything. As time has passed my time has become more valuable to me and my wealth has increased. I've weighed up the measure of time it takes to buy low, and now limit this to bigger items for big wins or 'giant leap gains'. In the past I'd spend hours and hours getting travel insurance for £30 instead of £45 from my local bank, or saving £30 on a new phone, putting a value on my time of sometimes £1. My Dad dies hard in me, but I have leaned the relevance of 'diminishing return on time invested', that my Dad didn't seem to understand. These days I reserve such endeavors to my PA or just pay the difference, getting involved in decisions that will have more effect usually focusing on making savings in the 4 figure plus range.

When I was 16 I would stand on a market stall selling socks that Sam had supplied me with in the freezing cold at 5am in the morning. I would then have people negotiating with me to get a £3 pair of socks for £2.50. At the time the difference this made to me was worth it and the cash I earned helped to leverage the money I make today due to the compounding effect that money has over time. I clearly wouldn't get involved in this now as it wouldn't be a great use of time. Equally I once spent four hours ringing eighteen insurance companies to insure my car to save £50 at 17. It was hours of speaking to people on the phone giving the same information over and over again. Not directly worth my time, but in the end I knew how the system worked and what does and doesn't push the premium up a lot. It would never be worth my time these days but the compound effect of doing this back then really pushed me on as I knew this knowledge would be useful later when insuring many Cars over the years.

# 16. Mark's guide to buying everything low

## Cars

If I acquire a new car, I will analyse the full cost of ownership over a 2 or 3 year period. If I bought it cash I will include my 'cost of my capital,' sitting in the car (at 5% a year), realistic maintenance, and the big one that most people don't see; depreciation. Certain cars can be very cheap to contract hire or lease due to plummeting demand in Europe for German models, and low interest rates. To keep the production lines rolling at similar levels, many manufacturers have performed market segmentation by pumping their cars out on extremely cheap contract hire and lease deals not seen before. Aided by very low interest rates, you can get £60,000+ cars for a small upfront payment (3-5 monthly payments, around £1,800) and as little as £350+VAT a month. With a deal like this there will be minimal maintenance costs due to newness and technology and ZERO depreciation (the invisible to most, overwhelmingly greatest cost with new car purchases). Compare the total cost of this brand new lease of a Mercedes CLS of around £10,000 over 2 years with owning the same car, bought new, where the depreciation could be £30,000 on its own over the same timeframe, plus 5% cost of capital at £3,000, road fund license, the list goes on. Here you have made an immediate saving of around £25,000 over a 2 year period, all in return for a little extra knowledge and a few hours 'work.'

Many people have a warped sense of 'ownership,' in that in 'leasing,' you never 'own,' the car. However in 'owning,' the car you 'own,' all the above costs. This is equal to a years' salary for the average UK worker, and £25,000 compounded at 10% over 20 years is £168,187. Isn't this mind blowing on one item? Imagine this across many of your purchases. I love this kind of leverage :-)

Just because you have to get a car serviced with the main manufacturer approved dealer to get the stamp in the service book, doesn't mean you have to get all/any other maintenance items from them. We run our Ferrari and other high end vehicles for the same cost of a quality German vehicle. Believe me, if you want to lose money hand over fist, buy a Ferrari and have it serviced the conventional, main dealer way. Most people go down this route because it is deemed 'standard,' but as with items such as printers, the vast majority of the money made in cars comes after the initial sale. Many dealer networks in the UK make little on the sale of a new car; the margin is in the maintenance and consumables.

I once took a high end German marque to a dealer as I wanted the stamp in the book for resale value. The cost of the service was £600, but they went on to inform me that a further £3,500 worth of other 'work,' was either necessary or advised. Many people accept this as they have little knowledge (or interest), but using my usual system I refused any extra work and sent the car to a local, independent high-end specialist. They still use all the same parts and have mechanics trained in similar dealerships as the UK manufacturer, but their prices differ wildly. I got a bill for £700 for necessary work on brakes and exhaust, which, importantly, I let them find and diagnose (i.e. I didn't tell them what the previous dealer had quoted). You will be quite amused at the difference in what garages tell you needs doing to a car, further highlighting that lots of unnecessary things are done. Not only do the smaller independents have a lower per hour rate, they keep the maintenance to more necessary items and mysteriously the amount of charged-for time it takes them is usually less than main dealers. This saving of £2,800, every one to 2 years, over 2 years at £5,600, compounded at 10% per year for 20 years comes to £37,673!

A Ferrari is not by any stretch the cheapest way to get about, but as it was bought at virtually the lowest point in its depreciation curve and 3 years on is within £5K of its purchase price, it's lost virtually no value. There aren't many cars you can own for 3 years depreciating at around 1% a year of it's new price, but we knew through research that certain marques start to appreciate, and most cars reach a depreciation floor that they don't drop too far below. Some even start to go up, and you can turn a passion/hobby into an investment (though this is specialist and risky for novices).

Being a low volume supercar, when things go wrong, which they frequently do, bills can be ridiculous. One particular example was when the gearbox went wrong (driving it less than 10,000 miles) and the local independent specialist couldn't repair it and, so it got sent to the main Ferrari agent. Because manufacturers have designed their products around making income from servicing and maintenance, a common way for them to stop non main agents being able to work on their cars is through selling the computers (that are essential in working on the cars) at an astronomical price to independent garages. As a different computer is then required for each make of car this makes it very expensive to service different makes of car. As you can hardly work on a car without the computer, they are able to exert monopolistic control of the market. This resulted in a quote for £15,000 to put it right. Please note that this wasn't even for a new gearbox (that would have been £25,000), it was for two new 'gears.' I went berserk. He'd had the car for months doing nothing. I pressed the dealer for more facts, declaring outrage. Shortly afterwards they revised their quote saying that two gears and a linkage change would suffice at £6,000. This one phone call and a non-acceptance of the 'norm,' saved me £9,000. Compounded over 20 years at 10% that comes to £60,547.

## Tyres

Consumable items such as tyres, especially on higher end cars, offer a golden opportunity to save cash. The way I drive erodes tyres at a faster rate than most, and a typical main dealer quote for two tyres would be £550 a corner (per tyre) for my car. Online, using sites such as my tyres or black circles, tyres of the same size, speed rating, section and aspect ratio can be sourced from cheaper manufacturers, in this case at £165 a corner. I'd burn four tyres a year, but if the car is new and I feel some acquaintance with the car is necessary, it will be six burned in a year! At a saving of £385 a corner, the total over the year is £3,300. Compounded over 20 years at 10% that comes to £22,200.

## Air travel

Business and first class fares are prohibitively expensive for most people. It's hard to justify spending £4,000 on a seat when you can get there in cattle class for £700. This is especially true for families where the extra cost for four would be £13,200 in this scenario, just for the flights to go on a decent long haul holiday. Being a complete aviation geek and loving anything to do with planes and helicopters, I started digging around forums set up so that geeks like me can devise ways around the system. After discovering the concept of an Amex British Airways air miles (Avios) credit card by a friend in our industry, I set about earning Avios points. Cards like this can attract sign up bonuses of 30,000 Avios airline miles after spending just a couple of grand, and even more by encouraging other family members to do the same thing and getting referral bonuses. We also had personal and business cards running tens of thousands of pounds through monthly which were earning no add on benefit, so these all got switched over. I was now in full geek-mode (it's often easier to get your families' agreement to set these accounts up then administer yourself or through your PA) discovering that the 100,000 Avios I needed to get to long haul destinations in a business class club world flat bed return seat could be quickly and cheaply obtained. My excitement apexed in unearthing that the Amex British Airways premium plus card has a once a year bonus called a 'companion seat.' This enabled me to take Gemma too (which of course I was not going to get away with NOT doing) at no extra Avios points costs; just taxes and sundries of around 1/8 of the cost of the club world seat. We now fly on £8,000 tickets for £1,200, a significant saving of £6,800. We now travel mostly first class only around the world, such is my addiction to finding ways of 'buying low,' miles. On our last trip to San Francisco we arrived for the usual £1,200 travelling on tickets that are over £12,000; a huge saving of £10,800. Compounded over 20 years at 10% that is £72,656. There would have been some inflation along the way, but once again isn't this mind blowing on one item? Imagine this across many of your purchases. I love this kind of leverage :-)

As big a benefit as the huge compounded cost savings are the time, work, health and energy related benefits. You save time not standing in queues that can be leveraged into research on your smart 'phone, you get complimentary food and drink in aircraft lounges conducive to relaxation and work comfort. You get well trained and attentive cabin crew serving you good food and making your bed giving you sleep and work benefits. You arrive fresh and ready for business and maximum time leveraged. Were I to specify and measure the time benefit of this it would be worth £10,000's to you. 1$^{st}$ class is also a great, higher echelon networking environment. I've met some great people who I still socialise and partner with to this day.

All the airlines are doing here is practicing a similar form of market segmentation that the car manufacturers implement. Many planes fly with empty seats, which the airlines would like to take some revenue for, rather than zero. Discounting these seats heavily will devalue the full fare, and over time the brand and perceived value of business and first class will diminish, ruining the service. These 'back door discounting', strategies are in most industries, and a little knowledge and research will sniff them out and utilise them for the low cost high life.

Over the first 3 years using this system, I have earned over a million Avios. To get a million Avios in the standard way you'd have to spend £1 million, but a little research and knowledge has generated trips around the world for a mere fraction of the total cost. Would I fly first class at £12,000 a pop two to three times a year? I think you know what my Dad would have said to that?! Not only do you lose such huge sums compounded over time, but where is the fun in paying full price?

I would be happy to send you some instructions on how to do the same thing. All I ask is that you let me refer to you one or two of the card companies I use so I get some bonus miles (and you will too) for more air travel. If you are interested email me at markhomer@progressiveproperty.co.uk

You have probably got the idea that I love travel. My early years of travelling around the world where Dad worked must be linked to this. His obsession with seeing new places and cultures has rubbed off on me. I also find that I come back much better focused on work and can get a lot more *effective* work done when I have had time away. I suffer from a mild form of SAD (self diagnosed), so the winter months can get me down. Getting out to somewhere hot for the New Year break has worked wonders for my mental well being, productivity and therefore wealth.

Skiing is another passion. Again Dad got me into it with a trip to Bulgaria, and after that I was hooked and have skied almost every year since 1993. A habit started by my Dad who took mum every year from the UK until they started living in developing countries.

## Interest

By having a great relationship with a bank or bank manager, nurtured for 3 years minimum, you will often secure lending cheaper than anywhere else in the market. A common deal for us would be to make this saving on a loan with 7 figures, and a specific deal I just did today was on a £500,000 loan. That is not just a £5,000 saving, it is £5,000 a year, for 20 years; totaling £100,000. There is on top the compounded effect of each £5,000 a year on that money, but to keep it simple, assuming simple growth for the first 20 and compounded for the next 20 years, 10% compounded growth on £100,000 is £672,000. Lets take that to the bank, shall we?

## Tax

Although not a tax specialist, time invested in understanding legitimate strategies and full utilisation of the allowances that the Inland revenue grace us (many fantastic ones for Entrepreneurs) is a great use of time, leverage and compounding. One great example is capital allowances on a property; a goldmine for the last few years. Pushing your accountant to learn and utilise all available allowances and structuring your investments in a way that is amenable to this end will be one of your best and most leveraged money saving/earning processes. The long term value of this higher level of knowledge compounds as greatly as the other strategies discussed. A pound saved in tax is a full pound in your sky rocket. A pound earned in your business is at best 50 pence in your sky rocket, net of taxation.

A picture of Gemma and I on one of these trips away flying first class using Avios

A picture of Mum and Dad on their annual ski trip, strangely in France – Dad
always went to Austria believing the German influence made them better
organised and respected their ruthless efficiency.

A picture recently of me in the Swiss Alps near Crans Montana.

## Computers & printers

If you are buying computers for your business, the lower spec £500 desktop with basic software package is ample and effective. Ensure a full five years use (three years more than most), replacing again with the equivalent (advanced) spec. This is much better than spending £1,000 (on a 'good,' one), as the small extra benefit this 'sssssstate of the art' (I can just imagine Chris selling these) machine provides from day one will be unnoticeable in months, and certainly in three years. In the second five year ownership term, the £1,000 machine will be drastically slower than the new £500 replacement machine. Across 35 staff, saving £500 per machine is a total of £17,500. Compounded at 10% a year for 20 years, this makes a difference of £117,731.

For personal computers (for you), I believe in Apple Macs. The reduction in maintenance costs, time cost of slow start up and shutdown, time offline due to malfunctions and general ease of use and intuitiveness, is all worth the extra cost. We haven't taken the step in the office because of the cost of capital on scores of machines and huge changeover period. Perhaps this will change over time if I calculate the need and net cost saving benefit. I have started testing with Rob, Andrew (our designer), myself and Katherine (our operations manager), and will glean more insight through 'Voyeurism,' over time. I'll keep you informed.

Printing is a major cost for most businesses. Your staff will be happy to press the button on anything, print off War and peace in Technicolor at 10p a sheet, and take little personal responsibility of the compounded cost and wastage. Our annual printing bill is around £15,000 based on a drilled down lease agreement and payment per sheet. If we followed the usual path of buying printers and getting cartridges from manufacturers, much like the car dealership, we'd have our pants heaved down. Printer lease companies can be negotiated against each other, especially as your volumes increase and the equivalent purchased costs of printing the same yearly volume would be around £30,000. If we could train our team to only print when needed, stay paperless and use the colour button sparingly, we might save another £3,000. Leaving that aside, £10,000 (a year) compounded at 10% over 20 years brings you an additional £67,275.

## Insurances

Insurance is a big saving opportunity area. Each year we insure over 300 properties as of writing, creating economies of scale purchasing power. The buildings insurance alone on this volume is over £42,000 per year. When you add in all other insurances such as car fleet policies, indemnity, employer and employees liability and others, we likely exceed £60,000 a year in basic premiums. By shopping around, getting new quotes every year and changing provider ever two to three years, I estimate we save in the region of £12,000 a year. It is a relatively simple process with a life-long upside and leveraged benefit. You can use my car research techniques from earlier in the book, ensuring you never believe/take the first quote, research in advance and use company quotes as bargaining chips. As an example of this, when I was searching for quotes for our first Ferrari in 2010, the first quote I received was £5,000. The next 5 insurers wouldn't insure a 30 year old at all on that kind of vehicle. Of course my experience and 'healthy skepticism,' kicked in, and I dug a little deeper. It was a relatively easy process to find a specialist top marques insurer who insured both Rob and I (and Rob had 9 points at the time, though he assures me he only has 3 points now!) for £800. This is an enjoyable saving for what is now a simple process for me, and will be for you too.

On another note for insurance, it is very costly to have more than 3 points, and your insurance premium will increase dramatically. It will save you significantly if you can learn to control your right foot and have a sixth sense for where officers of the law most frequent. It will also save you many thousands by racking up your no claims bonus, so regard these as highly as you would Avios points or money in your vault. Roll them up every year knowing you are saving and compounding, and if you ever have to take an insurance break, or you go on someone else's policy, it is often profitable to buy a £30 1 litre engined car and keep it insured, even if you never drive it, to store and compound the no claims bonuses.bv

An estimated £10,000 saving in insurance, compounded at 10% over 20 years gives you £67,275 to have working in your favour.

## Clothing

I use a time saving, 'silent compounding' strategy for most of my clothes purchases too. Although having to admit that Gemma is now my personal stylist, and having to wear what she places at the end of my bed each day, any opportunity to buy a years stock of clothes in one hit gives me a warm sense of fulfillment. A years stock of shirts at a Duchamp sample sale at the Music Rooms, or get a Bespoke suit at a local tailor for £300 - £700 instead of the £5,000 at Saville Row, is more than welcomed. Buying Jeffery West's at the Northampton outlet twice a year in their sales gives you a great British, well made show for half the price, and if you rotate you'll likely only lose £30 a pair wearing them for 3 years and selling them, as they have a 2nd hand value. Or you can get 10 good years use out of them. Trips to Bicester on new years day when it is the least busy, or online shopping at Secret Sales saves many thousands in yearly stocking up. Importantly, I must ensure that I am in one of these discount locations whenever I am shopping with

Gemma and my credit card is within 500 yards :-) I also get great benefit and enjoyment at doing this just *once* a year, stocking on full 52 week supplies, saving my valuable time which silently compounds, and keeping the painful experience of shopping to a once a year per item affair. I'm not sure how much you would spend a year on clothes, but if you're anything like my business partner or girlfriend it would be the value of a house! Let's assume a similar rate of spending/saving as the insurance, based perhaps on clothes for a family of four, and the compounded effect can be duplicated to £67,275.

## Watches

Watches are another source of cost saving leverage. I don't profess to be a world-expert, but have managed to invest in watches without any depreciation. Rob has a passion for watches like I do investing, and so is able to leverage a hobby he loves to save and invest. Although not a 'how-to,' manual in buying watches, it is universally recognised amongst watch collectors that certain brands hold their value and/or appreciate, and most plummet like a stone. The glitzy brands with high marketing budgets and big name celebrity endorsements that shine in the windows on the high street and pull in aspiring people to wear the watch to be seen in, rarely if ever appreciate. If you buy a watch from a company that has such huge budgets, you'll pay for their marketing, R&D and celebrity endorsements in the instant and continued depreciation. Brands like Omega, Breitling and Tag, although attractive and good watches, often drop considerably in value as soon as you walk out of the jewelers. There are a few exceptions for early rare 'Heuer,' or 'Monaco,' limited editions, or much older models with a very short limit of initial supply.

Many of the watches that don't drop (if you buy them well), or actually go up over time, are older, not as glitzy, or of specific model or type.

Most sports Rolex, especially steel Daytona's, many complication Patek Philippes, some Panerais like the 'Fiddy,' and some other more rare makes with strictly limited supply (AP offshore special editions such as the T3 or 'End of Days,') have shown historical growth that can be better forward-calculated. Some of these references may change, so do your own research. When you monitor supply and demand and historical price growth, you can gain extra benefit. At peak times, all-steel (not Gold or Bi-metal) Daytona's have up to a 9-year waiting list 'out of the window,' (new from the dealer) often selling at above full retail price. Some of the most expensive watches ever sold, in the £millions, are 1940's Pateks. If you gain a little more knowledge than others, you can go in low on a 'new second hand,' model (second hand but virtually unworn, normally by other collectors or aficionados) to a 'motivated vendor,' (think bankers in the banking crisis) pick up a Patek or Daytona at 10% - 20% off new price, then watch it grow at 5% or more per year (even being able to wear and enjoy it). Each year the major watch manufacturers put up their prices, sometimes more than once a year and often significantly, it bumps up the value of your much loved timepiece. The Panerai I currently have is nearly twice the price in the window now than when I bought it. If you build networks of high volume trading dealers in the UK and overseas, you can also get take advantage of currency fluctuations, buying from different parts of the world at the right time in the currency trade, buying at low prices and selling at high prices. You also gain from inflation protection, as the investment is not stored in cash. You would need to hedge against potential loss, so make sure your insurance covers you. Either enjoy trading watches, like upgrading your own personal home, getting free, zero depreciation use out of the best models, or build a large collection as an extended arm of your overall investing strategy.

I call this 'spend investing.' This strategy takes an area of your life where you would previously have 'spent,' money, and turn it into an investment. The compounded effect of this is huge, as one of the biggest 'silent,' Cancers of wealth is depreciation. If you have a Shoe, Handbag or Watch fetish-addiction, you can now lose the minimum depreciation, or even make small compounded profit. It is often worth 'spending,' a little more money, turning the depreciating 'spend,' into an investment. For example, if you have a budget for a £1,500 watch and can afford a Longines or Raymond Weil out of a window, delay the gratification for a year or two, and save up for a Daytona or other sports Rolex, second hand but with box and papers, for £3,500. In 10 years you will at worst have stored your money and protected it from inflation, holding or increasing it's value. The Longines or Raymond will be worth less than £100, depreciating by over 90%. On one watch this is probably a difference of £4,900, given that I'd expect even the cheapest second hand sports Rolex to be £5,000. There is another benefit to this I call 'wealth illusion,' that I will share in a moment. The compounded effect of £4,900 at 10% over 20 years on just one watch comes out at £30,099.

## Rates

On a recent property deal we are in the process of getting the rates assessed. We are challenging the rates that we pay on our offices with the valuation agency. Since 2007 commercial rents have dropped, giving an argument that many people are 'overpaying,' commercial rates at unfair levels. Of course the valuation office won't offer this information, writing to you with the good news of a bill reduction, they'll simply continue to charge you until challenged. Big savings can be made challenging these valuations, and in the same way empty property rates on empty commercial buildings. By taking advantage of exemptions to empty property rates (such as decommissioning works which is about to be converted into another use), can end empty property rates. The total estimated saving on 3 units in the current pipeline amount to £25,000. Compounded at 10% a year over 20 years you create an extra £168,187.

## Utilities

Big money can be saved on utilities, especially over multiple properties in the same way we save big on insurances. I like to call up a few major suppliers when it is time to renew and get negotiating. The last time I did this we saved around 25% over a standard one year contract price of an individual property. You can negotiate with suppliers when you have economies of scale. I often call them up using other supplier quotes as leverage and ask them to beat the quote given. Energy costs are spiraling in the UK amidst the government's green energy policy, where consumers have to pay a subsidy so the government can make feed in tariff and other payments to parties generating energy (from solar panels, wind turbines and so on). Because of this, big wins can be made with the understanding of this leverage and negotiating between big energy suppliers. A good way to do this is to look on the small business section of moneysavingexpert website, where the cheaper/cheapest providers at that moment are listed. Call them up, get the first one to quote, perhaps pull a 'little cheeky,' by taking a penny per unit off a previous quote, and name that quote to the next supplier. Watch them drop their rates quickly. On just the last 11 properties I moved over, with an annual usage of around £35,000 a year, the saving was around 25%, or £8,500. This figure compounded over 20 years at 10% is a tidy £57,183.

## Possessions

A great source of value or 'spend investing,' for possessions comes from auction sites, liquidation vendors and wholesalers. There are very cheap suppliers of furniture at wholesale prices that you can use for personal use, if you buy enough volume and are in the industry. My assumption is that, like me, you have a passion for property investing and see it as a lifetime investment vehicle, so you'll have no problems opening doors to wholesalers and trade accounts. The wholesalers I use for everything; flooring, furniture, kitchenware, lighting, fixtures and fittings, usually operate on (at worst) half of what you would pay retail.

Auction sites and liquidation wholesalers across the country are a great source for a value purchase. Let someone else lose half their money on the newness, VAT, margin to manufacturer and then liquidation sale price, and then come in and benefit. When researching you'll find some items are better than others, but anything that is not easy to transact (for example clothes of irregular size or large furniture items needing large delivery lorries) drop in price significantly, to be bought at less than 10p in the pound. If you find anything you like new, make it a habit first to search on these sites to see if you can get the same model cheaper (or even better) second hand. Although hard to calculate, I'd have to say that the total yearly saving using this model must be a minimum of £10,000, and the compounded effect over 20 years is £67,275.

**Refurbishments (Refurbs)**

This is the source of some of my greatest cost saving pleasure. In the last decade I have overseen the refurbishment of over 250 properties, but for this example I'll use your own home/private residence as the running example. Any small refurb jobs you undertake should be done by one man bands or loosely affiliated tradesmen. Bigger jobs will require a project manager and bigger teams, but be careful about hiring a major building company, as they will want big bucks to boot. One man bands are more negotiable, don't have staff, don't have overheads, don't have the ability to market themselves as well, and so need to take business when it comes their way. If they are new or in a new entity or don't do a lot of business, they may not be VAT registered. As you can't claim VAT back on residential refurbs, this is a particularly big cost/saving of 20%.

They key to getting the right prices for all your materials is by opening trade accounts. You need to go in to the wholesalers as someone who is in the trade, explaining to the person who opens the trade accounts behind the desk that you are a property developer refurbishing houses (which of course you are). Sometimes they will want to see an invoice or business card. A little 'cheek-creativity,' gets you a long way, but of course it is assumed that in reading this book you fit this ilk. Buying Kitchens at Howdens and Magnet you'll frequently receive discounts from retail of 75%. Flooring suppliers such as Karndean or local trade carpet suppliers will allow you to open trade accounts to save big.

Saving money gives me as much pleasure as making it. Remember that every pound you save is an entire pound, but every pound you make, 50% of it could be lost in tax.

If, when refurbishing your own home, you want higher quality items, outlets such as Porcelanosa have sales at 3 times in the year offering around 40% off retail. The accrual of all this should result in a greater than 50% saving of all materials. On a small rental property you should save £4,000 minimum on an otherwise £10,000 refurb, bringing it to £6,000. On your own home you should be saving in excess of £10,000. At 10% compounded per year for 20 years that's another £67,275 for you to enjoy.

Other huge savings can be made when converting commercial property to residential. You either pay 5% VAT or zero VAT on the conversion costs in this niche. Refurb men will invoice you for the full 20% VAT on these jobs automatically and the accountant won't notice. Its your job to show them VAT 708 (they usually take it to their accountant who then confirms its kosher) and they will often then only invoice you with 5% VAT for commercial to residential or HMO conversions. This will save you tens of thousands of pounds on the average pub or office conversion.

A nice little trick that the solicitor won't tell you about when you are buying a commercial building that has VAT on the sale price is to serve a VAT 1614D form

on the seller through your solicitor. If you are buying a commercial building to convert into residential rooms or flats, this allows you to dis-apply the option to tax on the building and pay no VAT on the purchase. This has another effect of reducing the stamp duty you pay on the purchase – yes you have to pay stamp duty on VAT on a commercial purchase if you don't do this. Most accountants and solicitors wont mention this unless you question them, so if you are in this market, which is a huge niche opportunity right now, do it and save thousands in unnecessary tax.

## General lifestyle

I use the same strategies for new contracts for mobile phones and upgraded models, getting low tariffs with big bundles and free new iPhones. The tricks to this are a. not getting the phone the day it comes out, as you'll pay a significant premium, price shopping with my research and power negotiation techniques shared earlier, and asking to be put through to the disconnections department if you don't make the progress you desire. It is at this department where you have the most negotiation leverage. If I'm buying a new sound system, I'll ensure I buy it at the right point in its depreciation curve, which in Hi-Fi and electronics often means savings of 50% to 80% in 3 years or less. With consumer electronics it is important not to buy too late in the cycle as the technology won't work, but, interestingly, it rarely does brand new, either. I made this mistake with Laser Disc, DCC, DAT, etc (if you can remember those 'next-big-thing home audio technologies that never kicked off, like Betamax or 3D TV). I implement the same strategy for wine and art investing; the list goes on because I have a somewhat OCD passion for it, and because I can just see the pound signs rack up through 'silent compounding.' Just totaling up what could be realistically measured, in one standard year living in the world I experience, owning a house and car, doing a house refurb, making some investments and renewals and buying your usual quota of possessions, the total saving in that year could be up to £258,700.

And the total compounded saving added together over the next 20 years is a staggering £1,791,735. This shows how you can become a realistic, bona fide and sustainable millionaire in your lifetime just by saving on unnecessary spending habits. This has not even factored in reinvesting and multiple re-leveraging. If you did, and added in all the figures in this section for travel, Cars and so on, the figure might conservatively be £3million to £5million. I like to call this 'silent compounding.' Every day, every penny saved is getting bigger and bigger and bigger, especially if re-leveraged into assets. Most of the outside world can't see this, and so it is your strategic advantage. It's what you can't see, the intangible, whirring away silently in the background like a Dynamo, that makes much of your long term compounded wealth. I hope this illustrates my geek-fuelled obsession of cost saving and compounding, why I love it so much, and how you can become a genuine, everyday, non get-rich-quick-scam, sustainable millionaire. All it takes is small, consistent and disciplined behaviour in the present moment, managing of the short term retail therapy emotions, and my parallel universe thinking technique.

## Parallel Universe thinking

If you are unsure in the moment of the right compounded investment decision, or you feel the urge of retail therapy emotion rearing its ugly head, implement this simple, 10 second technique that will aid your long term, low cost, high life. As you are trying that article of clothing on in the changing rooms or looking at the new 5D TV that makes your breakfast in bed, take 10 seconds to ignore all peer pressure, emotion and sales assistants, and set up two universe scenarios: universe 1: you buy the thing and it depreciates to 1/20th of its value in 15 years. universe 2: you don't buy the thing and the amount you didn't spend goes into an asset compounding at 10% a year, and giving you a 5% income at the end of the term. In the scenario of the '58 inch smart TV', this is how it would look. Universe 1: £2,000 turns into £100. Universe 2: £2,000 turns into £8,354 and produces a yearly income of £417. My guess is that in any year you could have dozens of opportunities to implement 'parallel universe,' thinking to 'silent compound,' your way to a job replacing passive income and pension replacing asset base for a sustainable low cost, high life.

## Don't get divorced

If you want to maintain and compound your wealth, do not get divorced.

## Wealth mirage

Wealth is as much a perception as it is a reality. I actually get as much personal benefit from the appearance or small taste of wealth as I do the opulence, which can often be a let down or over striving for the next, bigger, best thing. Wealth is an impression, a perception, as much a judgment by others as a feeling in yourself. As much as I'd love to write that what others think of you has no importance, and that you should just 'be yourself', if you want to progress in business and investing, the impression you make on the people you meet is as leverage-able as 'silent compounding.' Business is about relationships and connections, having mentors, experts and technicians in areas you have no knowledge or experience, and magnetically aligning them to your vision and legacy. And if they think you are a skin-flint, like I've been chastised the odd (few thousand) times, then your road to success is longer and slower.

Many of my wealthy friends and partners lavish opulently on potential clients, partners and mastermind peers, and I have witnessed it working to powerful effect. By in true low cost, high life mantra, there is a smart way to do it on minimum budget. Some ways to create the wealth mirage; the appearance of wealth for the short time it is needed, are:

## A driver

Hiring your own driver is actually quite an investment, despite its lavish appearance. The time you would be driving could be invested into asset research, purchase or management, and would pay a compounded return. To begin, you don't have to hire a full time driver, just a driver for long journeys that you can't take the train, where you could be performing income generating tasks instead. You could start with a family member or friend, and build up as the demand creates. The 'wealth mirage,' to peers or mentors that you have a driver is positive, and most people I know of real wealth have drivers, so it puts you in a higher echelon by association. If you have important clients or partners, 'send your driver,' to collect them (not in your £46 brown Nova) and you are likely to create the impression that gets you closer to wealth.

I have recently found a superbly leveraged luxury boon called Uber. It is a tech company that operatives a service that you use through an app on your phone. It connects you to luxury chauffeur driven cars in capital cities. Its brilliance is that it is an on demand service that allows a huge number of chauffeurs on its service who are in (say London) to get jobs near to their location. This keeps them constantly working with no 'void,' periods. They therefore don't have to make an empty return journey which costs you more (private hire cars in the UK aren't allowed to pick up passengers who aren't pre-booked).

The result is that for around the same cost as a black cab, you can have a Mercedes E class (with suited chauffeur) take you to your destination. Pay a little more (say 1/3 extra) for the "Lux" service, and you get a long wheelbase Merc S class or Audi A8 with a chauffeur who stands to attention and opens your door; a service fit for a king. The value of this when meeting certain clients can be huge as Rob and I experienced as leaving a meeting of industry entrepreneurs recently when we walked out to the car to be greeted by Vlad in front of our industry colleagues to get into a £100k Merc that we paid £14 for our trip to Kings Cross station in. The Ferrari would have been the wrong image. That's Low cost high life :-)

### Michelin (equivalent dining)

Many people budget on eating out when on tightening the belt, but this can be false economy, especially when you have an important peer, client or mentor meeting. Many a business deal is done over fine wines and small but artistic portions; so take the best people to the best places. If you make a local restaurant your regular establishment, the service will be impeccable, you will have a heir or royalty, and you may negotiate 20% plus off the usual price. Often the finer the restaurant, the more courses you have and the longer it takes, so you have 'bought', more time to work your relationship or salesmanship,

## Luggage

A good laptop bag and holdall are important in the 'wealth mirage.' You are being watched and judged. I am not talking about being a celebrity and spending £5,000 on a Louis Vuitton suitcase set showing how many times you can print the logo on one item, more a subtle showing of class. Go for a recognisable brand like Tumi, Boss, Paul Smith or Gucci, and find the equivalent lightly used on Ebay for 1/4 of the price. I believe this to be an investment, and I don't like spending money, in case you hadn't got that picture.

## Premier banking/cards

Premier services at banks have many benefits: no queuing, relationship manager, breakdown cover, travel insurance and more. For the very small charge, just a few pounds a month, this more than covers the cost (especially if you run a Ferrari through the breakdown cover!). In addition to this, you have the 'black card,' that looks more affluent, and you have a higher identity around the dinner table. You need to earn a certain amount for these, though I've known them to be relaxed with their qualification criteria to win the recurring income business.

## Airline Lounges

The higher echelons of these airline lounges can be accessed for not a lot through using Avios and flying Club World or First Class on British Airways (or a one world Airline). Especially with the first or Concord lounges, there is an exclusivity created by the fact that airline tickets that allow you into these lounges usually cost in excess of £4,000 per seat. Well out of the reach of most people, you can access this level of luxury (the Concord lounge is probably the best in the world) for around £600 a seat on long haul. You will mix with those who have often paid full price taking you into a different network. My Dad would have been proud but probably would have stolen all the free food!

## The best of the important things (one item)

You may remember my Dad having the very best of each/one thing, and storing it to occasionally look at. This pornographic enjoyment I never understood, and you could take it one stage further and actually use these items, getting material benefit. If you buy one pair of cuff links, a Handbag or shoes, a tailored suit (with 2 pairs of trousers), a shirt, overcoat, wallet and so on, then you have the 'wealth illusion,' without over spending. Choose each one carefully; not too overstated but recognisable, and research for the lightly used prices online at up to 75% off. Use these for all important occasions and they will pay a passive return on investment. You can do this for your watch too as detailed earlier.

## A PA/VA

At Progressive we've trained thousands of start up Entrepreneurs to build their property and business empire. On almost every occasion, taking the step up from one man band to employer is the biggest single hurdle. They see it as an expense they can't afford, or have misconceptions or bad experiences on hiring and managing people. I believe you can't afford *not* to hire a team, as there's only so much one individual can achieve, no matter how super human they may be. The 'bridge,' to your 1,000 strong workforce bringing you in £10million a year is not as hard or risky as you might think. In the new world of social and technology, we are instantly connected. People the other side of the world with a lower cost base and income, or stay at home Mum's wanting to earn extra money flexitime are the perfect type to help you with your admin and non income generating tasks. You can start on a per hour contract, only paying for consumption. Even if it's only 5 hours a week, those 5 hours re-invested into income generating tasks will kick start 'silent compounding,' and your income will rise. Time is the most valuable resource and leverage-able asset, use it wisely, it will pay you the most interest. A VA (Virtual assistant) needs no office, desk, employment contract or training and management; just clear instructions on tasks to free your time.

I don't know anyone in my wealth circles who doesn't have a PA. The perception of having PA is that you are executive, and you have a real business. If you didn't, you'd be almost instantly boxed as a one man band; and to be seen to manage your own diary or admin would be frowned upon. You could further leverage the 'wealth mirage,' by having two or three (though of course not sharing they do 3 hours a week each), and even name them as your executive assistant. Richard Branson has 12 PA's apparently, so the measure of your perception and income would be relevant here.

## A private plate

A private plate that covers the age of your depreciated Car can create a powerful 'wealth mirage.' If you choose wisely, and go for a 6 or 7 digit plate, it's not likely to cost you more than a few hundred quid. A well chosen one will probably appreciate too, so if you can choose one that may have a common market, it can be an asset too. I'm not suggesting buy

A1 for £200,000, just a small investment to further leverage perception.

## Your language

Language is possibly the most immediately accurate signal to your knowledge and experience. 'Oui,' et 'non,' wouldn't be enough to get you by in France, and so a lack of financial literacy will expose weaknesses. If you speak to any well experienced and wealthy Entrepreneur/investor/ business person, they will use the language that is known in their niche, through experience. It's almost like a code or a Peacocking technique to exhibit power, education and heritage. You can shortcut these decades of experience by learning the language; financial and business terms: vertical integration, PnL, balance sheet, fiduciary, top heavy org chart, depreciated asset, gross margin, cost of sales, you get the picture. I recommend buying 'Naked finance,' a great book for non-finance people about finance; then spit out some of the phrases like they were the first words you learned as a baby to create a grand 'wealth mirage.'

Please note that creating a wealth mirage,' is not creating a 'wealth illusion.' you are not tricking anyone or being a fraud, you are simply 'being it before seeing it,' or helping build credibility for yourself. You know the difference between perception and illusion, so I don't need to patronise you.

Rob and I have both passed our PPL Helicopter exams to become private helicopter pilots; another great 'wealth mirage.' The challenge for most people is that this really is very expensive. Pretty much indefensible in terms of wealth creation (Choppers have the opposite effect), we hire rather than buying one. Until you are at 200 hours flying a year, it doesn't make financial sense to buy one, and they drop like a stone (I would have enough paper to draw a depreciation curve) and cost a bomb to maintain. If you can request flying lessons for every birthday, Christmas

A picture of me in the Robinson R22 (and R44) we fly.
Please note I am not as smarmy in the flesh as I look in this image

## Gifts

There are many smaller but still valuable areas that you can leverage. I love buying gifts for people; it makes a great impression and warms your soul. I recommend that if you are not feeling good, buy/give/offer a gift to someone; it's the best way to make yourself feel better. When buying gifts for people you want maximum 'gratitude leverage,' for minimal cost. I did try buying second hand Handbags for Gemma on Ebay, but this didn't make the grade so will omit gifts for loved ones from this section; I don't want to be referenced in anyone's divorce papers. However, when buying gifts for birthdays, Christmas, partner and mentor thank yous, clients and so on, using online sites such as secret sales and subscribing to independent high end brands gives you the best sales tip-offs, before the mainstream population. I calculate that over the course of a year I will buy gifts in the region of £10,000. Using private 'sample sales,' and buying in January sales 11 months ahead of time will save you at least 50% of this figure, in reality more like 70%. You can either buy gifts that are nearly 3 times as good and enjoy the extra 'gratitude leverage,' that it brings, or pocket the £7,000. Compounded over 20 years at 10% that comes to £42,897

## Nearly 30 lessons by 30 - Summary

The ultimate luxury in life is getting to do what you love to do every day. Ensure your standard of living is not equal to your cost of living. In the world of business and property, patience pays. Buy them and hold them. Invest in something you can fully understand. Look for opportunities most people are put off by and take your unfair competitive advantage. Never get too involved in management. The real payoff is finding others to do the work, while you watch the P+L and balance sheet. Don't compete to the point where you're trying to hurt people, you're not out to destroy the competition, but forcing them to raise the quality bar. Don't overstretch on liabilities and always buy at a reasonable price.

# 17. Nearly 30 lessons by 30 (part 2)

## 17. Assets & liabilities

I have a golden rule in investing: only buy/pay for big depreciating liabilities with income from assets. If you buy big depreciating liabilities with capital, it does the opposite of preserving it; it erodes it. The fastest way to poverty (even despite a large salary) is by depreciating your capital. Remembering that cash/capital preservation is rule no.1. If you desire liabilities such as cars, possessions and even holidays, ensure they are funded by assets and capital is preserved.

A simple single let investment, net after costs, should return a minimum of £150 per month. Staying at this safe figure, if you desire a £45,000 car, you either need 25 years of saving from one property, or 25 properties of the same type, to reach that figure in one year. Or you could finance a lease payment of around £300 per month given in the earlier example. If you need £1,500 down, then 10 months of net income and you have your deposit from one rental asset, and 2 rental assets will meet the monthly lease/contract hire payments. Although it would be technically incorrect to say you had the Car for free, it's as close as, and you have paid for 2 years use of a very nice car, funded totally by an asset that is appreciating in value with zero erosion of capital. This is the lowest cost way other than a lottery win to finance a depreciating asset. Those 2 assets could fund leases on Cars for the rest of your life.

If you use this strategy and mentality to purchase most, if not all of your depreciating possessions, you will never erode capital. This 'asset backed purchase,' strategy is also like setting a goal or challenge to achieve something of merit in your life, and it always tastes so much sweeter. It drives you to focus more on investing in assets and adds to the magic of compounding that we've already illustrated. It's a smarter way than saving for something then buying it cash to avoid debt; something that might have been smart 35 years ago, but now only really means over delayed gratification and under leverage of capital and debt.

## 18. Watching the pennies

It is easy to only focus on frying big fish, but there are sayings about watching the pennies. I utilise a strategy, that I have for over a decade, where I save all spare change and coins into a failsafe container anyone (especially me) can't easily remove. Once every two years I bag it all into a coin machine, take it to the bank, and once the right investment comes along, transfer/invest it in. A simple but compounded benefit. Rob does this with what he calls his 'Lady Godiva's' too, saving his £5 notes in the same way. This strategy alone could give you enough passive income in your lifetime to replace/pay your living costs and personal overhead.

Every year in April, and only once a year, I go onto moneysavingexpert to look for the highest paying savings account (based on instant access), usually with a bonus that lasts a year. I usually transfer any cash holdings or money sitting between property purchases into the best offering. All banks, like insurance companies, are built around giving you an attractive level of interest if you are a new customer, only to then drop the rate, often at the end of the first year, through removing a bonus, defaulting to a lower rate or other mechanisms. By the end of that year you could be at 0.1% interest, which if you have a fair capital sum is expensive. Though a bit of a faff, it is essential to do this every year. Diarise it now. If you benefit to the tune of 1.5% on £100,000, then you know what happens to that amount when compounded over 20 years.

## 19. Net worth monitoring

You can only master what you measure. The two critical measures of your personal (not business) financial position are your net worth and monthly income (from all sources). Knowing these are the only way to compare year on year progression (or recession). Your net worth statement gives you net equity in all assets (I like to deduct sale costs too), including cash, properties, stocks, watches, bonds, ISA's, and, importantly any negative equity assets (they should be included and not deluded). Diarise each year half a day to recalculate these, ideally over the xmas and new year period in an exotic location to inspire and motivate you for the next year, and keep a past log of each year so you can see the growth tracking back from the start, year on year.

This can also be a cathartic process. A friend of mine and a partner in one of our businesses, Unlimited Success, showed me through his old journal that he started in 2005. He has now made a seven figure sum, and we both enjoyed reading in his journal his initial goal to 'make £1 online.' When you track back through your goals and net worth statements, you see for real how far you've come and you can leverage that sense of fulfillment (or pain if it's gone down) to attack the next year.

## 20. Return on invested time

A main difference between wealthy mentors I have and poor people is how they 'value,' their time. The wealthy spend their time on tasks that generate strong income ('giant leap,' tasks) or make huge costs savings, and are able to delegate lower value tasks that would keep them poor. Too many people are doing too many low value tasks to be rich, and working too hard to be wealthy. The wealthy don't sweat the small stuff. Sometimes old habits die hard and you could find yourself scrapping with someone over a fiver, but as you go up the value chain you realise you can never get that time back, and it costs you significantly in opportunity usage. Your net worth in these moments of opportunity usage actually dips down (invisibly), so focus on high value-to-time-ratio tasks as much as you can. Your measure of progress will be in spending more time on bigger projects with bigger wins and less on admin, minutiae or low income generating activities. You should delegate, outsource or hire for these tasks, investing a small amount to free your time to go for the higher echelon of time remuneration.

### 21. Thinking big vs. cutting your teeth

To understand how big deals work, you need to understand the costs at a more grass roots level. I am all for thinking big and I'm sure you've read endless books on this subject, but there is a balance of progression that is the least risky. If you rent off your Mum at the age of 65 and the first property deal you are doing is a Casino, thinking big will be more akin to delusion. Conversely, if you never take a bigger step up into the unknown, inflation erodes all your progress. Think big but start small. Start small and safe, and test test test in a protective environment. Importantly, just before you're fully ready, but once you've analysed all risks and costs, go to the next level; just a little above your comfort zone but not on another planet. You'll find there are as many new things to learn as there are similarities, but at least it isn't all unknown and you can balance the experience you bring from a previous deal with the desire, hunger and necessity to learn the intricacies of the bigger deal.

Good boxing promoter/managers know this well. If a talented boxer breaks on the scene, the temptation might be to give him a fight against the current Mike Tyson. This could ruin the young and talented boxer's career, as a big knockout causes emotional as well as physical damage. The smart promoter gives the fighter a couple of easier 'journeymen,' fighters to build confidence, then creeps them up with fighters with more experience but perhaps less talent. Perhaps it might take 5 years plus and 15 or more fights to get your big title shot, but this strategy will give the fighter the best chance of a world title. Then once they have the title they have to defend it against the up and coming rookies.

## 22. British mentality around wealth

A lot of what could be improved about the UK (in my humble but perhaps irrelevant opinion) is the envy that many people hold towards the wealthy. This manifests itself in many ways and is cyclical and topical, aligned with the events of the moment. Banker bashing has been a recent fashionable sport, along with outrage at big multi-nationals who pay less tax because of the way in which they're (legally and entitled to be) structured. People would do far better, be much happier and far wealthier by trying to emulate the way wealthy business people have generated income and assets, rather than stand against them to make themselves feel better about their own position. The politics of envy can be very destructive and push those very people further away from wealth. The 'tall poppy,' syndrome in the UK prevails in many poor circles, and I think it's a waste of time trying to convince people who are 'happy in their misery,' to change. It is far easier to gravitate towards new circles giving full immunity from other people's insecurities or biased beliefs.

We have experienced this envy locally and on forums, in the media and channels that allow protected expression. I am actually surprised at how little of this we have encountered, and assume it will only increase in volume (not necessarily percentage) as we grow. Whilst this envy used to upset me, and I used to take it quite personally, I now realise it is a cost and privilege of doing business, and a measure of your brand. Much like celebrities won't read the lies written about them in some newspapers, I won't read certain media if I think it is biased, based around envy or a pity party union. I make a point of cutting out people like this from my life, and as a result over time I experience this less than I thought I would.

We admire great artists, amazing athletes and genius minds in our society, so why not admire those who are the greatest at attracting wealth more? This is more normal in the US. Notice that if you ever feel this envy or insignificance, as I must admit to feeling in the past, it is usually a reflection of what one is not happy about within themselves. Have the strength and personal awareness to catch yourself out and change your thinking. If you don't or can't, accept a life of wealth mediocrity.

## 23. Pricing

Less experienced Entrepreneurs will get sucked into price competition too early. The only way to create more sales or a market advantage (in their mind) is to drop the price until they get custom by beating competition on price. They then end up selling their £10 product for £5, which anyone can do. These are the people you want to be buying from, like the refurb one man bands mentioned earlier, but not if you're selling. This reduces margin (sometimes to zero or less) and teaches the market of your value, attracting the penny pinching customers you don't actually want, repelling those who want more value. This effectively cements your low position and becomes your brand.

When you are pricing your own products or services, this is ill advised. It is a myth that people buy on price only. You should differentiate your products, services and consultancies in the marketplace by increasing (perceived) quality, increasing (perceived) service, increasing the (perceived) story, increasing (perceived) benefits and other factors such as 'ego-value,' (cosmetics, trophy real estate). When doing this you increase the *value* and *perception* significantly, and the result is that you attract those who perceive that extra value as something worth paying for. These, interestingly, are also the kinds of customers you'll find the easiest to deal with, give you the least grief and probably cost you the least. No one who wants to buy quality will buy cheap, so being cheap repels the best customers.

People naively think that a market has price restrictions. In almost every market I've researched, the range from cheapest to most expensive is huge, and when an impressive player comes into the market with an amazing product or service, they themselves can reset what is an expected level to pay for the item. A good example of this is/was Dyson. Before the Dyson (and the cyclone technology), who on earth was interested in spending upwards of £350 on a vacuum cleaner? No one would dream of it but the very wealthy. A vacuum cleaner was an operation tool of necessity, not a symbol of class and identity. However with great technology, marketing and a great 'story', the bar was totally reset and almost overnight people saw it as a 'necessity', to spend four times as much for a vacuum cleaner that did exactly the same thing. This example is similar with the story of Apple and other quality, disruptive brands who recreate the norm by shaking up a tired or monopolised industry.

Your personal (or company) confidence in your product or service (or lack of) may end up being the biggest determining factor in your price strategy. Rob often refers to Tracey Emin and Damien Hurst, artists at the same time as him charging and making millions for their non-labour intensive works of 'art', yet Rob, stuck in his house for days on end putting 100's of hours into each piece, selling virtually none of them. His experience in business has now told him that other factors already mentioned, especially marketing and story, drive the price up. Most importantly, he simply didn't have the confidence or belief to put the high price tag on. And you won't get many people asking you to pay 50 times more than your price tag.

## 24. Productivity

Possibly to your surprise in a book called 'Low cost, high life,' exercise and health management are in my view the keys to wealth productivity. Running 4 times a week for at least 30 minutes to 70 minutes (or desired equivalent), at more than 70% of your maximum heart rate, will aid your wealth attraction. I also limit alcohol consumption to a maximum of 2 glasses of wine (or the equivalent) a day, not more than 3 times a week. I also make sure I eat light salads at lunch, as anything heavy or carb-filled effectively writes off the next three hours, costing many thousands in the moment and many tens of thousands compounded over 20 years. I personally function on a whole new level of focus, productivity and energy when I stick to these rules, and importantly, I don't make bad, reactive decisions because I feel good, or worse, in order to feel good. It seems like there is a birthday or anniversary in our office daily, and if you ate a piece of the celebratory cake each time you'd be dead in a few years!

Mornings can be very productive before other staff members, emails and interruptions from others pile in. If you're in an open plan office get some earphones and block out background noise. People will soon get the idea around you that you're not open for inconsequential chitter-chatter. Rob goes full extreme on this with his HUGE Denon 'can,' headphones. One look and it is clear interruptions will not be tolerated.

I barely answer my phone other than to people I know or important calls, and most frequently respond to voicemails or email, as I can choose the right time to respond in a more concentrated way, without the inefficiency of needing to re-engage my brain back into the topic I was in. Or I can delete, which is often the best strategy. Being chased by the demands of others can waste hours per day, and vitally important or high income generating tasks can be interrupted, delayed or even forgotten. Most sales and admin calls can be dealt with later if they're important. I make a point of unsubscribing to emails I'm not interested in anymore, freeing the space in my email inbox, and not replying to calls that have not left a voicemail.

Remember that you control your time, not other people. Without the necessity to be rude, your face needs to inform that your time is valuable and that you can't be interrupted at certain times. If you don't teach people your rules, you'll be ruled by theirs. You'll have certain work flow zones, individual to you. For some it is first thing in the morning, for others it is in the evening. Find yours where you feel the best and achieve the most, and ensure all high value tasks are performed, in an uninterrupted fashion, in this time. It then won't matter if the rest of the time gets wasted. It's actually a great strategy to waste time and procrastinate on tasks that are not important.

I learned a lot about productivity and lack of from the way that Chris used to work. He'd constantly interrupt me whilst I was in flow or doing something important (most of the time for him), for something so small and irrelevant, because he felt the instant need or caffeine compulsion. Many of his bad decisions were in the energy gulf just before he'd connect himself intravenously to the Coffee machine. How you manage your time, life and energy relate very closely to your wealth and income. Wealth relies on smart, well balanced decisions. I'm sure your personal relationships are at their most positive when you are feeling full of life. Ensure when making investment decisions you are in the same zones, and put off and de-prioritise fluff into your crash zones.

## 25. Net Time & Leverage

A lot of people fool themselves into thinking they're busy, when in fact they're busily ineffective. Many people 'actively procrastinate,' staying 'busy,' to convince themselves they are 'working.' Effective, wealthy people ensure maximum productivity through leverage of time, tasks, money, contacts and expertise.

### Task leverage

Any task you engage in needs to be income generating to the extent that it makes a positive financial impact in your life (or has the potential to). The tasks where you have the biggest opportunity to create 'giant leaps,' forward should be reserved for you/your time. All other tasks that most people get stuck in and busy with such as admin, ineffective research, emails, taking unimportant calls, tidying the office, should be outsourced or delegated to others ('leveraged') at a lower (opportunity) cost. This doesn't necessarily mean you need huge payroll overhead if you're starting up. A virtual PA (VA), a friend, a family member (Mum's are great!), a contra-swap of free services, or even your partner can get you over the bridge.

Accuse me of being un-PC (put it on the feedback form!), however I have a deal with Gemma that I don't do any cooking. She cooks three nights a week and the rest of the week we eat out and I pay. This saves me hours of tasks which I am not good at, I don't enjoy, and where I could be doing high income generating tasks. She gets her dinners paid for and the relationship is fruitful and loving because of it! When we go on holiday, her job is to wash, clean, prepare and pack all clothes and items necessary for the trip. My job is to pay for the holiday. She'll cook a couple of times, though this often gets replaced by a sunset dining experience (I finance). The reality is that she is far better than these tasks than me. If I iron or pack items, it will look like it has been run over by a Lorry. She is also way better at picking colour combinations for me, and so she chooses clothes for me. She enjoys this deal we have, and despite what the ladies reading might be thinking about the relationship and it's 'traditional' nature, it works very well for both of us, makes us both happy, and creates value for us. The hours I save can create tens of thousands of pounds of income, and only cost me some dinners and a couple of holidays a year, so a good financial investment return. And eternal love, of course :-)

Although simplistic the example is, it is important to take this methodology in every business and investing decision you make. If you don't enjoy the task, or it is of low income value, it will cost you money, or you'll lose money, by doing it. People naively think they will save time by getting it done themselves, only to waste hours bringing in zero income. A PA is one of the best investments you can make, in case you haven't got this message yet. Apparently it takes 10.2 times to make a message turn into an action, so there are another 7 chapters on hiring a PA/VA! My PA opens all my post, manages my diary and responds to any letters or appointments that don't generate me income or give me a 'giant leap,' in progress. She books travel and holidays, tickets, social outings, she does research, manages email and keeps the gate; all for a yearly salary that I can pay in 1/5 of a single property deal. People resist leveraging to staff, PA's and VA's because they think they can't do it as well as them; they may as well just do it themselves. In the short term this may be true, but as long as your staff (PA) stay around long enough, the time invested in training them to be as good, or better still better than you, then lower value tasks will be done quickly and efficiently at a small investment, and 'giant leap,' tasks will get done by you. You'll also start to see more opportunities come your way because now you're not too busy with your head in a Rabbit warren digging deeper and deeper, to spot them.

Did I tell you that you should hire a PA/VA? Or even twelve?!

I used to buy all our (and our clients') properties entirely myself, managing the entire process start to finish. Sourcing, purchasing, refurbishing, renting, managing. A decade ago these were 'giant leap,' tasks for me, and well worth my invested time. Now it is an operational task that keeps me from growing the business and doing larger commercial projects. It was essential therefore that I create an hierarchy/org chart and purchasing/management system for the entire buying process: someone to source (using my systems), someone to progress the sale (using my systems), renting the property out (using my systems) and managing them on an ongoing basis (using my systems). Of our 40 full and part time staff, we now have 6 people in the property acquisitions team implementing the systems I created by going through the entire process myself for many years. As staff have come and gone, and we've held on to the very best, the *systems* have continued to get the results. We are also de-risked from illness, staff leaving or other 'irregular shocks.'

## NETime

NETime is a valuable way to manipulate time and create extra leverage. My favourite method of this is to take the train or my driver (Rob's Dad) where I can when travelling. Instead of driving, if you get driven or take the train, ensuring your environment is comfortable and conducive to work, you can utilise this time 'already spent,' to great effect with 'giant leap,' tasks and double leverage. If you get an hour's work done, you effectively leverage otherwise wasted time therefore creating an extra hour in the day. It also makes the otherwise boring journey go a lot quicker. Pinching a couple of hours a day using this technique, when compounded over 20 years, creates an extra 14,600 hours in the two decades. Imagine putting all this time into 'giant leap,' tasks.

Other strategies I love that give this great benefit include using the handsfree kit in your car and booking all your important calls into the journey, one after the other. You could also listen to powerful training audio in the car, or in the gym, or whilst running. We have many of these on property and personal growth in our companies if you should need some to get started. I like to run with Gemma and Margo (our Labrador), which is effectively triple leverage. I've walked the Dog, spent time with Gemma AND done my daily exercise: saving me two hours in the rest of the day to focus on 'giant leap,' tasks. Most people whine that they don't have enough hours in the day; smart people create NETime.

This book is an example of NETime. Creating the time to write this book, not naturally in my flow, would have taken a year or more. NETing this task with an 8 day holiday is the best (perhaps only) way of getting this beast of a task done. It's made it enjoyable, creative and achievable, and of course turning down an extra trip to the west coast of Barbados would be crazy, right?

Amongst many other things which she has brought to my life, Gemma really helps me to focus on what I'm good at, with her taking up the slack in other areas. She is a superb host, soul mate, very kind and supremely loving. Having her in my life has helped my mental well being and happiness hugely; she helps me to concentrate on business and making money as I have such a happy home life. I would recommend you find a good man or woman to get behind you in what you do. They need to be on the same page and supportive of your business and wealth creation habits, if they are not they will be a serious impediment to your success. She didn't ask me to write this part either!

### Tech leverage

Technological advancements make it easier than ever to NETime. If I'm ever stuck in a queue or forced to wait on hold on the phone, or any other dead time, this can now be leveraged on a MacBook Air, iPad or iPhone (yes, or Android or Samsung!) with a Wi-Fi connection. You can access all your work folders remotely, emails, calendars, all bank accounts (I can access over 200 bank accounts remotely), contacts and my diary from every corner of the globe, even on your Yacht in the middle of the ocean. You can 'pinch,' hours a day of 'giant leap,' tasks whist living a highly enviable, low cost, high life. Make sure you invest your time in technology that saves and leverages it. Deal analyser Apps (search 'property app,' in the app store), task managers like 'Evernote,' CRM systems like sales force, email marketing systems like Evernote, webinar/online training apps like Gotowebinar, audio and dictation apps like Dragon, even health and lifestyle apps like myfitnesspro. Of course as I write many more will come out, and others in your specialist niche.

*Staff leverage*

Creating an org chart with tiers of management will keep you moving to higher 'giant leap,' tasks. For you to keep moving to higher 'giant leap,' tasks, you need a bigger team. A PA will serve you well, but you can't run a multi-national £billion enterprise with the two of you, so creating levels of management is key to your continued growth. Importantly, it takes the management of the team away from you, as any more than around six people managed by any individual will become difficult. It will enable a large team to operate and prosper without your time input, or at least keeping it to board and strategy meetings. Managers can be held accountable by managers at a higher level and a superb opps manager, as we are fortunate to have at Progressive, will keep the team effectively performing as one, and growing according to your plans and vision. This creates massive leverage and continues to advance your 'giant leap,' tasks.

The hiring of talent is possibly your most important business priority. People are the biggest asset in your business, so make it your income generating focus to build your power team of the most talented people you know. This is not a recruitment book, I'll leave that to the experts, but I'll tell you that as we have grown this has become our focus more and more, and is a strategic not operational 'task'. Have your talent radar on full at all times, and when you meet great people, enthuse them with your vision and hire them. I recommend Nolan Bushnell's audio book called 'Finding the next Steve jobs', for finding, hiring and managing the best (often difficult) creative talent.

I know many people who have hope of a 'Laptop millionaire', lifestyle of having no team, no staff and no problems, sipping Sangria on the sunny sandy beaches smoking cigars. This is a pipe dream. Look at *any* major company that turns over many £millions, how many of them have no staff? The wealthiest individuals often have the largest teams. In fact it is recognised that for each member of staff a business has, you should pull in around £100,000. The maths is easy on this basis.

### Cash leverage

My most favourite leverage is that of cash. Investing through your lifetime getting returns only on your own cash would be too slow to build serious wealth. In fact, we'd probably have a mere dozen properties by now and no more, had we had to buy all our properties for cash and have the cash sat 'stuck' in them. Money from banks, equity partners, joint venture partners, bridgers and private financiers all help you 'leverage', to invest in income producing assets. You might only need a small percentage of the purchase price (anywhere from 0% to 30%) and these financiers will lend the rest secured against the value of the asset; in most cases property. As long as the net result is that the repayment (or interest only) of their loan is covered over the period in income (rent), and all your other costs too, then you are effectively paying back the loan for free, owning an appreciating asset. Of course, you'd be looking at getting some income yourself on top, and it is quite plausible that you could expect anywhere between 1% and 8% net after all costs including finance (gross 8% to 15%), on an asset partly or entirely funded by someone else. This represents a far higher 'return on your cash,' and is effectively 'leveraging,' income from the financial partner you have.

Over time, if you accrue the income you can re-invest that in much the same way, creating 'leverage on leverage.' You are also likely to get capital appreciation if you have the assets long enough (or in short windows in the cycle) that you can 'refinance,' and re-invest in the same way again, creating more leverage. After your initial start up leverage, every deal 'stacked up,' afterwards becomes infinitely leveraged, in that you have used profit from a previous deal. This is a most exciting concept, and how we leveraged the ability to buy 20 income producing properties in our first joint investing year (Rob and I), into many hundreds. To many this may seem risky as you are borrowing money. What if the tenant doesn't pay or you're left to pay the mortgage? What if interest rates shoot up? These are variables you can quite easily de-risk by choosing the right investment types, in the right areas. As long as these assets are carefully and diligently managed and protected with the right financial products, they will set you apart from other novice investors or speculators.

Over time, as you build relationships with lenders and financiers, the borrowing will become more predictable, liquid and cheaper. Not only do you leverage their funds, you now 'leverage the relationship,' benefitting further to produce more net income. They'll start to 'lend in lumps,' wanting to give you your 'free,' lending in high six or 7 figure tranches; enabling you to leverage the time of applying for multiple small loans. You'll also find they start chasing you to meet their lending quota; I found it exciting (and ironic) that after my early days of begging banks, they are now begging back. I am happy to help them meet their targets, of course.

## 26. Commercial property opportunity

If you have enough knowledge and a nose for an opportunity, you'll see many over your investing career as the cycles cycle and the opportunities rotate. Sniffing out the mould from the Gold will be down to your instinct, intuition and experience. It would be impossible to cover all of these in this book, and they'd change over time anyway. One that is most noteworthy, however, and making us significant wealth now, is the opportunity in commercial property.

Right now commercial property is at about 1/3 of the cost to purchase second hand, as compared to the cost of building a new unit from scratch. This is fire-sale cheap. An example being a recent acquisition, with a 2007 sale price of £1.7million. This is a £160/foot purchase cost, and to build it would have been £1.3million. We acquired this same building for £350,000, or £33/foot. This is 80% less than it was sold for in 2007!

The main reasons for these bargain prices are an oversupply of offices in many town/cities, especially older than 1980's units in need of upgrading. Getting long leases, even finding tenants has been very difficult. Many companies have closed down post recession, people have been made redundant and a more mobile or working from home lifestyle in today's age has evolved.

The demand for residential property in the UK is still very high despite the recent crash. Bar the problem with banks/lending (that is showing signs of recovery as I write), people still want to buy and rent houses and flats and the demand for this is increasing. There is a huge shortage of residential properties in the UK, and this has been prevalent for many years (research 'Barker report'). As developer volume has reduced through the credit crunch, big opportunities to develop/convert commercial property into residential have emerged.

With conversion costs in the region of £50 - £60/foot on projects I'm involved in, and purchase prices of £30 - £35/foot, a healthy margin is realistically achievable. As the government want to promote this activity to put empty commercial units back into use, ideally in a way that helps them with their housing shortage problem, there are many significant tax breaks and planning changes to help you make an even bigger margin. If you are converting non-residential buildings into flats for sale, you will end up paying zero VAT on conversion costs; a significant saving. On flats that you hold, you will incur just 5% VAT on the conversion cost.

More recently, the government has removed the necessity to apply for planning permission in most areas on these building types. Office (B1) conversions into (C3, usually flats) require no planning permission; merely a much smaller 'prior approval,' process. This speeds up the process considerably, reduces development risk, saves tens of thousands of costs, and most importantly there are no section 106 contributions or affordable housing to be provided. Translate: expensive taxes. On a 13,000 sq. foot building, a community infrastructure levy for example could be in excess of £50,000. Even more burdensome would be the affordable housing obligations which a site like this would bring, which could run into the £100,000's, making developments like this previously untenable.

Because these changes are very recent, the early mover advantage for those well positioned is immense. This is an opportunity that if it sits somewhere between 'Thinking big and Cutting your teeth,' for you, that you will profit handsomely from. This is a great example of an opportunistic 'giant leap,' contrarian task.

# 18.Your (personal) Investment strategy

Getting great results in all asset classes is either virtually impossible, or takes decades. It would be far wiser to focus on a single strategy, becoming 'active,' and the very best at it, and having a more 'passive,' strategy for the remaining classes you'll store and grow your wealth within.

A 'balanced portfolio strategy,' relies on your main active strategy (for me this is property and business) and a diversification of other strategies that vary on the scale from 'active,' to 'passive.' The class you have the greatest passion and enthusiasm for, such that it doesn't feel like work (and one that is leverage-able) should become your single main 'active,' strategy.

When you become great at your main strategy, not only will you make direct income and equity in that main class, you'll discover other 'cross-stream,' opportunities over the years, and 'bolt them on,' with relative ease, further leveraging your experience and results. In property an example of this in Progressive was the relatively fast set-up-to-profit bolt on of 'Progressive Lets.' Had we tried to set up a Letting Agency in 2006 when we had less than 20 properties, we'd had been spread so thin and had a significant knowledge deficit that we would have likely failed, and/or jeopardised our main focus of our own portfolio.

Once we hit over 250 properties in a joint venture portfolio, setting up Progressive Lets already had huge leverage. It had a quick jump-start of 250 properties to manage, and after the initial challenge of transferring them over, was profitable in quick time. Had we started our Letting Agency from scratch whilst we were heavily immersed in buying ourselves, it would likely have taken 5 years or more to get to 250 properties, assuming we didn't implode through overwhelm and exhaustion. It took us 3 months to get to that level when we implemented the 'cross stream,' technique, leveraging our existing portfolio that we did quicker because we focused on that. Initially decide on your main strategy that will create these 'bolt on,' opportunities over time.

This main strategy should involve buying low, leverage and cash preservation. Your aim should be to buy low, leverage the finance of others with minimal (without undue exposure) cash input. A good purchase price discount or some growth over time will allow a refinance of your asset to draw your own capital outlay back, restocking your cash pile. This will allow you to grow an asset base whist preserving and even growing your cash pile. This is not possible in every asset class, which is why property is my preferred vehicle. Your cash pile creates buying power and protection. Of course this brings the problems of inflation erosion, cost of capital and bank security, so it's important to spread that cash pile into other liquid assets, or use it as a recycling mechanism to purchase cheap assets when they get passed your way. This 'liquid cash pile power,' means you can finance the best, cheapest deals because the best deals often need cash purchasing, as financing takes too long. This doesn't have to be your cash (leverage). Cycling this cash across liquid assets protects it and gives a return whilst it's waiting to do its real job (protection and buying power).

I like to invest up to the ISA allowance per annum into the stock market. If holding or trading stocks was my 'active,' vehicle, it would be much more, but it isn't. I plan to grow this taxable allowance and never spend it, as the income it generates over time can fund a passive living. Please note this is *not* to trade. Trading without expert knowledge is gambling. The ISA's are spread across multiple equities and bonds usually through a fund structure and therefore de-risked, yet liquid enough for an emergency. The compound effect of this strategy gets better every year. I often use 'random cash windfalls,' (the more that comes in the more you implement 'silent compounding'), dividends or salary income in excess of living expenses for this.

A further arm to this investing strategy is taking bargain stock opportunities as they arise. I don't usually "trade" these but invest spare or un-utilised cash into a company that is fundamentally solid, with a strong history of profitability. Usually it that has run into what I would determine as short term troubles (or seems undervalued meaning I invest on a mean reversion basis). I will try to target companies which I judge to have strong cashflows from products or services that I understand so that I can better predict likely demand for these into the future. I will then focus on companies which have had a run of negative press, the effect of this is inevitably to push the stock lower making the company cheaper. As many people are influenced by this bad news and sell they sometimes forget that the media doesn't determine the long term ability of a company to make decent profits. The companies with underlying strength (and they by no means all have this) will get through their issues, the news will turn positive again and the stock price will rise as people buy making a profit for those with foresight.

It is important to 'pound cost average,' when stocks are a little volatile. This is a technique to buy the stock in stages, gaining an average price over time and spreading risk. I'd say I make a handful of these investments over the year. I don't like investing in volatile companies with little heritage, but prefer safer bets such as banks who've run into what I see as short term troubles. Remember that this is not 100% fail/fool proof, even banks and insurance companies go bust, as we now know all too well.

Then you have a physical arm in your investment portfolio, such as gold, silver, watches, art, wine and (classic) cars (the right ones). Once again the investment in these comes from cash lumps (dividends, big deals etc) or 'random cash windfalls.' I prefer not to hold huge amounts of physical due to storage and insurance issues, but in times of serious currency devaluation or high inflation these become more valuable. If you spread it across a variety of media, you are de-risked from big fluctuations, loss, damage or bad decisions. Physical assets don't produce income so are one-dimensional investments, relying purely on 'buy low sell high,' and capital appreciation, but they protect cash in severe circumstances. Their liquidity varies too, so spread to gain 'cross section benefit.' A niche classic car or piece of art is not as liquid as Gold that can be taken to a London broker and immediately sold.

I would regard business as an investment. It is likely to be the biggest cash producer in this strategy. Business is most likely to produce much of your income to diversify and implement all of the above. A solid long term business will often be sold at a valuation in excess of 3 times profit. Friends of mine have sold businesses in hundreds of millions and I got a billion dollars often on very high multipliers: 40 plus times turnover in some instances, making 3-10 times profit is a reasonable valuation for many solid businesses. Not being a 'trader,' of businesses, I see them more for income than asset value, and would consider a sound business as the main asset in any investment strategy. Once you have one main business asset, you can implement the 'cross stream,' technique to use the leverage gained to set up other, add on businesses that take much less time. You can use Progressive as a good example, starting as personal buying for Rob and I, cross streaming into buying for clients, cross streaming into property training, cross streaming into a Letting Agency, cross streaming into other companies. This high life all started with no cost just under a decade ago, and you can do it too, perhaps in a shorter timeframe by leveraging the knowledge and experience in this book.

## The wealth pyramid

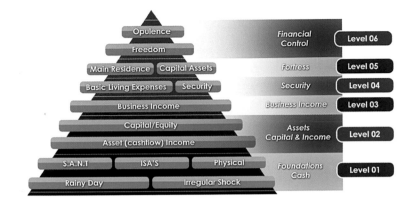

This wealth pyramid shows how you build layers of wealth. Most people think that six minutes of work will bring freedom, many only dream of opulence without the foundations or actions, and the rest think it can't be done. They just don't have a plan or system.

### Level 1.

Wealth is built on solid, unbreakable foundations. Foundations must be liquid (easily accessible to protect against unknowns). Therefore 'Rainy Day,' is money set aside, probably in a 'high interest,' yet instant access account (or stocks or bonds that are liquid), that can be instantly accessed for rainy day needs. 'Irregular Shock,' cash is for the things that come out of the blue that only hurt if you don't have the cash (boilers, big bills, major car or house repairs etc).

'On top,' of these are invested cash 'assets.' S.A.N.T is S.ave A.nd N.ever. T.ouch; cash that you put aside but never, ever touch. Yes never. Why? Because one day you will be able to live off the income it produces. Plus if interest rates get high in the future while the rest of the UK are hurting you'll be holiday-ing. It doesn't really matter how much when you start, as long as you start. I have some money attribution (bucketing) rules a little later. This cash can go into bonds or stocks or the bank. ISA's speak for themselves; ensure you invest the maximum allowable, tax free amount each year, and again, never touch it. There are now some 'ISA millionaires,' people who have now got £1M plus through investing in their ISA's each year. This will provide a good steady passive income. Physical is tangible such as gold (Bullion, Krugerrand, Britannia), diamonds, watches etc. Physical generally become more valuable as currencies devalue, or you can use them to 'trade,' against currency fluctuations. These are less liquid but build your wealth battalion.

### Level 2.

Once the immovable foundations are set, you have your asset level (cashflow and equity/capital). It is not essential that you only focus on level 1. before building level 2. Equity assets include physical (level 1.), certain (classic) cars, property, art, wine, stocks etc. Cashflow (income) assets include property, stocks and bank accounts if interest rates are high.

### Level 3.

A great way to build equity and income is to build (a) business(es). Business income can actually tick the boxes of all types. It can produce income for you through salary, dividend or drawing and it can have equity value (upon sale) that can grow significantly. Level 3. can be started immediately and doesn't need to wait until levels 1. & 2. are fully set.

Once you have set levels 1. to 3. you have multiple streams of passive income as well as a strong asset base that can protect from crash market cycles and drastic regulation changes.

Everything above level 3. is now recurring, passive and protected. This is where you have a sustainable low cost high life.

## Level 4.

Basic living expense covered by the assets beneath them, so you are not relying on a salary, exchanging your time for money, or exposed to feast and famine income. Security covers all main living expenses with enough left over to live a humble, comfortable lifestyle. You never have to work again.

## Level 5.

The fortress level is where you have your main residence(s) fully paid off. Whilst I don't like idle capital not being leveraged, for most people their primary residence is their single biggest lifestyle expense. So to have it unencumbered keeps living expenses trim. It is a very secure feeling to know that you have no mortgage, a luxury most people only ever get late into retirement.

I recommend getting a drawdown facility so you can have your residence(s) paid off but draw it down if needed when a juicy, discounted asset comes your way. You can also trade your residence up every 3-7 years as the property market rises, paying no capital gains tax, for 'free living.'

## Level 6.

Once all the level beneath are secure, you can do what you want, when you want with who you want. You can travel the world, make flippant decisions and enjoy material items knowing that in the next 30 days or less the income you indulged in will drop right bank into your accounts. Then you have a no cost high life!

## Income Bucketing

In order to have these layers of wealth full to the brim; you need to be disciplined and strategic with your income. You need a plan for every penny. This system below will give you a sure-fire way to sustainable income, silently compounding and growing the longer you implement the system. This system never decays when followed religiously; it just gets bigger and easier.

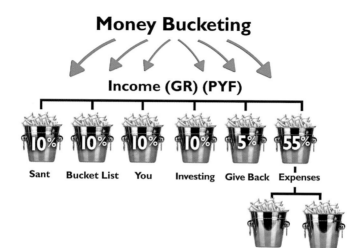

## Arrows at the top:

The multiple arrows denote multiple income streams (gross – GR); you can build up to this, even if you only have your job to start with. If, when you start, your living expenses are at 93% (instead of 55% or lower), then do two things immediately:

1. Shave your expenses down (I'm sure you can get them down to 80% without too much sacrifice)

2. Apportion the remaining percentage accordingly and build up to the percentages in the money bucketing visual.

## PTL:

One of the very best advantages of running a business is the taxation advantages; they are numerous. For all that we rant about taxes and the government, I am very grateful for all the opportunities and advantages to the Entrepreneur, investor and business owner. After all, it is our endeavours that pay most of the taxes to the central government (VAT, employers and employees national insurance contributions, corporation tax, business rates). As business owners, we fund most of the public sector, the government know this, and so allow the business owner to *PTL* (Pay Tax Last). A beautiful concept.

## *PYF:*

An employee doesn't get their salary. An employee gets a slip with the perforated edges, opens it like a golden ticket, only to see the top number eroded by tax, NI and student loan. They end up with around one third to half of the top figure; known as (not much left to) take home.

But a business owner gets to collect all the income. They can even add VAT on and hold that in their bank account for the three month period until it is owed. They can run all the legitimate expenses through (that you can research on government website public domain), and pay tax on what's left. There are many allowances and company structures that allow you to run cars and other high expenses through. Of course the finer details are for a good accountant. They get to PYF (Pay Yourself First).

## *S.A.N.T:*

Save and never touch, as discussed in the wealth pyramid

## *Bucket List:*

You might think it strange that someone of my upbringing would attribute money into a 'bucket,' bucket; income for your bucket list. The things to do before you die. But as I have released the shackles of my Dad's upbringing I have enjoyed life a little more, and too much delayed gratification means no gratification, and then death.

I've also found that forcing myself to spend some income on rewards;

things that give me pleasure and gratification, become self fulfilling and motivating to do more. It drives you and you end up bringing in more income for the other buckets (with discipline of course).

## YOU:

The YOU bucket is for self investment: you are your best asset, you pay yourself the best interest, invest in yourself wisely. Courses and training, networking, research, experience, mistakes, books and audio programmes, masterminds, lunches with big wigs, mentors and mentorships; all an investment in the asset of YOU; probably the most important bucket.

## Investment:

When you start, invest 10% of your income. You now know exactly how to do that. As you build your wealth pyramid, increase the percentage in the investment bucket. In fact, as you grow your wealth you can increase the percentages in all the buckets, except tax and living expenses, which will go down.

## Give back:

Rob and I have given a few hundred thousand to charity; and whilst it hurt at first ;-) it is cathartic and soothing. I am sure you believe in good karma and want to help people, and I think it is important to use some of your wealth to do good and make a difference. It feels great. It makes you want to earn more so you can help more.

## Top 5 for wealth leverage

As I use this book to reminisce over the last decade I realise we did well fast, but you can do it faster. Wealth works best the longer that 'silent compounding,' has been in effect, but that doesn't mean it has to take forever to achieve your low cost high life. The single most common question on wealth and success I get it 'If I/we were to start again, what would I/we do differently?' Here are my top 5 answers to give you the maximum leverage to get started or to take the next level up form today:

1. Hire staff quicker, especially a PA and operations manager (MD, CEO)

2. Implement the 'wealth mirage,' strategy earlier. My under confidence in the earlier days inhibited this

3. Become an expert in one thing as quick as I could

4. Use the naysayers naysaying as leverage

5. Focus on raising finance (JV's, relationships, mindset of money, leverage) more than low value tasks

## Your (personal) Investment strategy - Summary

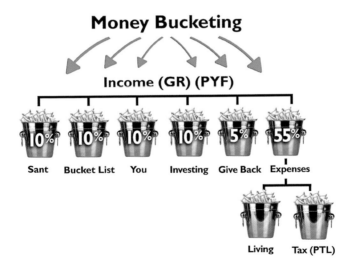

Think mid-long term. Will any investment decision aid your sustainable success? If something seems too good to be true then it probably is, so walk on by and leave the gambling to the gamblers. Stick to your strategy

and be forever wealthy for generations to come. Don't be lured or tempted by anything that glistens or is coated in chocolate. Become an expert in property (or your chosen niche) and you will be successful. Alternatively find an expert and leverage their skills and experience and you will fast track your expertise. Only listen to those who've done it and actively hunt them down then (in a nice way that leaves them feeling good) suck them dry for their experience. Buy them lunch or whatever it takes ☺

# 19. And Finally...

## Conclusion

I hope you have got a flavour of how my view of investing works and what I believe you can do to supercharge your low cost high life. I totally believe that anyone can follow these strategies to become a long term success with enough wealth to create your ideal lifestyle. The main ingredient of a successful investor or business owner comes in the form of a truly ingrained deep passion for the 'sport,' of making money, helping people, solving challenges and being in the game. The more you can make this part of who you are and surround yourself with the type of people that enjoy this pursuit just like you, the more successful you will become. There are literally hundreds of different strategies and businesses which can become the vehicle to get you to the net worth number you crave, but it's the craving that needs to burn deep inside you that makes the biggest difference. Once you have got it, and you can learn it if you want it, it will endure and push you through adversity, failure and any other challenges the market can throw at you. It will push you to view another property or find another way to fix a problem in your business or get another customer in when many wouldn't bother. Find out what type and style of fuel (business, property, investing) your fire runs on and feed it until the fire is white hot, and the low cost high life will look after itself. I wish you all the best in your journey and hope that we get to be part of each others' high life.

For more information or help, feel free to contact me on any of the details below:

My email address: **markhomer@progressiveproperty.co.uk**
Company website (property): **www.progressiveproperty.co.uk**